WALKIN

in the

NEW FOREST

by

JOAN BEGBIE

*With 16 illustrations from photographs
and 25 drawings by the Author*

IN THE HEART OF THE FOREST

PREFACE

OUR love for the New Forest is much greater than our knowledge of it. This being so we can only hope we have got the names of its woods and hills, its moors and bottoms aright, or, at worst, that we have made no mistake serious enough to lead a reader far astray. But if we have, and he should lose his way on our account, we comfort ourselves that wherever he may wander in the New Forest he will find beauty waiting for him.

ACKNOWLEDGMENT is due to Messrs. Judges, Hastings, for permission to reproduce the Frontispiece and the illustrations facing pages 16, 32, 40, 80, 92, 128, 144, 176, 184, 224, 256; and to Mr. C. Toomer for the illustration of 'The Sporting Pig'.

The map which is reproduced on the end-papers has been supplied by the kindness of Mr. Sumner.

CONTENTS

ILLUSTRATIONS

CHAPTER I

A PRELIMINARY
CANTER

W<small>E</small> think it is splendid country for walking, that is, for our own particular kind of walking, which is of a leisurely 10-mile a day kind, requiring only normal garments and no accessories. To walk as we walk it is not imperative that I should cram my unsuitable feminine curves into shorts —those eminently male garments—nor don ankle socks, nor arm myself with a cross between an alpenstock and one of Harry Lauder's comic supports.

We are not long-distance hikers, and though it is possible easily to map out hikes of 20 or 30 miles or more in the New Forest we prefer a 10-mile stretch which avoids as much as possible the retracing of our steps.

It is therefore as hardened 10-milers and also as explorers that we set out upon these wordy walks, for we *are* only exploring as yet and so at the most enjoyable stage of any walking.

All three of us love the New Forest for reasons which I now set down. Bill finds it a paradise for perambulation because here as nowhere else he can indulge his passion for natural history untrammelled by keepers. Mr. Bundy revels in it because here, and here only, is he practically certain to meet no motors. I delight in it because it is free and beautiful and there is such a lot of it, and it is still almost the same as it was before the Romans came.

Where else would you find 100 square miles of fine country open to all? The New Forest, covering nearly the whole of south-west Hampshire, is a playground where anybody can walk, sleep, and eat without fear of interference so long as he behaves as he would expect any rational

2

being to conduct himself. Only if he wantonly damages trees or allows his camp-fire to get out of hand will he fall foul of the verderers and their henchmen.

Speaking broadly the country lying within the watery embrace of Southampton Water, the Solent and the Avon, and rubbing shoulders with Wiltshire on the north, is nearly all free country where rich and poor are equally welcome. A good many acres are privately owned and on them ' the curse of the pheasant ' has fallen, but the great mass of hill and moor and wood is as yet untainted by snorty prohibitive notices and belongs to the Crown, or in other words the Nation.

When we first came to the Forest I was rather disappointed, as I believe many have been before me. In the words of two footsore American ladies I once gave a lift to, I cried, ' but where are the trees ' ? I did not know then that ' forest ' means a wild, uncultivated country as well as a wood and I was unprepared for so many miles of moor and plain.

But Bill adored it from the first. From the moment he leapt out of the car at Picket Post he realised he was in the promised land, that here was the country where a naturalist of his bent could live and die happy. The breeze greeted his quivering black nostrils with the age-long challenge of scent flung carelessly to every gust by deer, fox, badger, rabbit, water-rat and all. Rejoicing he accepted every gage, scouring away with flapping ears and head erect in ardent quest of the challengers who, I am glad to record, have never had cause to regret their defiance. Bill, I should explain, is a bull-terrier and Mr.

3

Bundy a rough-haired brindled griffon of diminutive size and choleric disposition.

As we live in Ringwood, once a beautiful old market town but now invaded by bungalows and villas, we have as a rule to get into the car or board a friendly 'bus when we start out for a day in the New Forest, but there is one walk we can take from our own doorstep which leaves not much more than a mile and a half of traffic-ridden highway to negotiate.

A gravel lane, beginning well with the Stuart manor-house and its enchanting stables on one side and a charming old house called The Elms on the other, runs under trees and past a row of painful nineteenth- and twentieth-century habitations and stops at Northfield Road where the road joins the Salisbury highway. Immediately opposite, near a garage, is a field-path.

The field will shortly, I understand, be groaning under bungalows, but up to the present it has either been at one or other of the stages of corn-growing or peopled by fat and friendly cows when we have walked across it. Out of this field the path enters another, and then another, where for a while it wanders hand in hand with a hazel-shadowed, golden stream where trout are to be found. The stream has an open bay where dogs like to swim and where children with glass jars, bare legs and infinite patience, catch minnows.

Once I saw a kingfisher dart across this bay and speed a dim, blue flicker up the dusky hazel avenue beyond, and once—oh! memorable day—I surprised a great grey heron at his fishing. He was standing under the bank and did

4

not see us coming until Bill came floundering down it into the water. Then he rose and flew majestically away, allowing me a good view of his black pigtail, long yellowish rapier-like beak, and his cold round eye. I have seen him here once or twice since, but he is trailing his long legs over the hazels before we can get close. .

Herons, I was told by a local country man, are bad things to meddle with, and was given the following story as an illustration. One cold, foggy day a man returning from duck shooting heard a curious noise in the fog above his head. He was anxious to learn what the vocalist was and chanced both barrels at the place he judged the noise to be coming from. There was a cluttery rustle and down came tumbling the awkward body of a heron. The man ran up and stooped over it to pick it up, but like a flash the dying bird drove its beak into his face and the poor fellow went home without the heron and minus an eye.

The path crosses a stile and a wooden bridge over the stream, with a big hanging bramble bush by it where Bill searched long and diligently for a rabbit who stole out between his hind legs and hopped leisurely away without disturbing the hunter. Right-handed and into the next field, and the pine-topped fringe of the Forest comes into view. This field has a little scrubbed oak with a hollow in it which is just like the oak in the Baxter print called the Love Letter, and in Spring the daisies there are a joy.

At the next stile the path divides into two, one branch still following the stream, the other cutting boldly across the big, rough field strides across a gravel lane into another field, turns right at the stile, runs over a third field and

5

a green lane, and into another field always misty with a lovely mysterious-tinted feathery grass, and so out into the Moyles Court road.

But I have overshot the mark, for on this walk we turn to the right down the gravel road when the path leaves the big, rough field. It was in this field that Bill killed a black rat, the only one I have ever seen.

The road joins the Moyles Court road about a quarter of a mile below the place where the field-path enters it and climbs a steep little wooded hill. Left at the top and we are out on the lovely stretch of open heath called Rockford Common.

Beyond on the right are the oaks and pines of Redshoot and Great Linford Enclosure; in the middle distance are the pretty little whitewashed thatched cottages called New Buildings; ahead are the distant slopes of Ibsley Common, topped by the neat plantation of pines called Whitefield Clump, which is one of three planted by the second Lord Normanton in 1835 to give variety to his view from Somerley House, and to act as landmarks to the traveller; beyond it to the left is the Avon valley with Somerley woods and the sober white house where hang so many good pictures, and beyond again the hills of Wiltshire and Dorset.

Goats are tethered among the gorse bushes on the common, ponies and long-legged Forest cattle with clonking bells graze here, and on lucky days the thoroughbreds of a Ringwood butcher go streaming across it with the ease and grace that only their kind possess. No deer, no greyhound, no leopard can come anywhere near their

6

exquisite, effortless rhythm. Rabbits there are in plenty, and Bill, whose hunting is of the haphazard variety, stumbled upon what must have been a half-wit member of the family, and actually caught it. In the flush of victory he turned a somersault over his prey and it escaped him. Having told two tales against Bill I feel it only fair to tell one against myself. I too somersaulted on this pleasant common, coming rapidly off the back of a three-year-old Forest pony whom I was taking for his first walk abroad. The fault was mine (also the pain), but he, being the most saintly of all ponies, waited for me to remount, thereby heaping coals of fire on my head. Circumstances over which I had no control, as Mr. Guppy would say, obliged me to part with him and he is now a most popular guest at a livery stable in Lyndhurst.

Rockford shared with a few other high and heathy places in the Forest the privilege of being looked upon as a health resort for bees by the local hive-owners, who used to send their hives to the Forest when the heather was in bloom. They would be taken in charge by a forest beemaster who placed them in earthwork enclosures and saw to it that the ponies and cattle left them undisturbed. It is over 100 years ago that the last bee family packed its trunks and set sail for the heatherlands, but on Rockford, at Hive Garn Gutter, and on Ibsley Common the little earthen breastworks of the bee-gardens are still to be seen.

The common is crossed and recrossed by tracks, but we go with the main track which drives right across it and plunging down past a group of pines at the end whose

7

branches one May day shook out three cuckoos as we passed by, joins a gravel road, which climbs quickly up by the group of cottages called Linwood, leaving Appleslade wood on the right, and so under the trees at the top and onward too far for us to follow to-day.

We leave it at the top of the hill and follow a track that runs off to the right. Hollies and oaks roof it for a few yards and then it trickles across a tiny green circled by trees and through a hatch gate guarded by Roe Cottage. Through the gate is Roe Wood, and to left and right are Milkham Enclosure, Redshoot, and Pinnick, joined ultimately by the Linford woods.

To be worthy of the freedom of the Forest you ought to be eager to know all that you can about its woods, moors, and bogs, and though, as I have already said, I do not know much about them as yet, I shall lay what little I do know before you hoping that it is accurate and that you will be interested. Most that I have learnt I got from the books of Mr. Sumner, nearly all of which I have at one time or another borrowed or bought, on being told by those who know that he is the best informed ' Forest lover ' living—and what pleasant reading they are !

Roe Wood, then, was planted four years before the battle of Waterloo. It is a delicious wood with a stream, the Linbrook, running through it, and its oak trees seasoned here and there with fine sweet chestnuts and a pine or two ' to taste ', growing close together above bracken and thorn. Foxgloves grow high and beautiful here, and near the stream towards the lower end of the wood wild columbines prink and preen.

8

Redshoot and Pinnick are ancient woods, and being so disdain the interloping pine and the dago sweet chestnut. Stout old oaks, thorn trees, hollies, and crab apple reign here supreme.

Milkham is the plain one of the family. It is a war victim, for most of its trees, pines planted in 1861, fell by the axe and became pit and trench props during the war. To this is due its ragged appearance, its sparse population of pine and self-sown oaklings, and the big, bare patches of coarse, yellow grass. However, it has its compensations for it is the cradle of the Linbrook.

All these woods are cut by rides in all directions, every one of them good following. We take the centre gravel track the gate opens on. Down this track when the meet is at Roe Cottage come the gravely-trotting hounds escorted by huntsman and whips in scarlet or green coats, according to whether the pack is fox or buck, and down it now flies Bill and disappears into the bracken ready to follow whatever may offer. And what a golden chance there is here, for these are the woods beloved not only by the little fallow deer but by the lordly red deer himself. Mr. Sumner has actually seen red deer here, and in the rutting season has heard their challenging roar come tumbling down the glades.

Mr. Bundy keeps close to me as he takes his duty as escort very seriously, but occasionally he makes darts to the roadside uttering little sniffling whines when the sound of Bill's hysterical yelpings announce the get-away of some quarry, or when an inviting whiff almost overcomes his loyalty. That he longs to be off I am certain,

9

for if I make Bill walk to heel to cool down a bit Mr. Bundy is into the bushes in a second. He has no nose to speak of as far as appearances go, but no tyke living or dead had a better nose for scent or followed a line more surely.

The track swings delightfully up and down, crossing the stream on its way, and we stay with it until just before it leaves the wood to debouch on to the heath called King's Garden. Here we take a green ride to the right which turns us out of the wood and into a gravel track. The track immediately steps over a trickle of water on its way to join the Linbrook and proceeds to negotiate the heathy ups and downs and the bogs of Buckherd Bottom.

At the top Mr. Bundy turns spiritually pale and I call frantically to Bill, who after some minutes comes tripping up with yards of dripping tongue falling out of his jaws, his white coat streaked with the black and yellow mud of the bogs, pretending that he has only just this minute heard my voice. Quickly I snap the leashes to their collars, for skimming at dizzy speed across the skyline is the ever changing army of cars whose joy it is to race along the intoxicating Forest roads.

The track joins this speedway at a point called Handy Cross, marked by a pond usually attended by a group of Forest ponies.

Courageous or foolhardy beasts they have no respect for the knights of the road, though this summer alone, on this one stretch of road I have seen two full-grown members of their tribe lying dead on the grass verge after contact with motor-cars, and have come across a hideously

10

mutilated filly foal struggling and slipping on the tarmac
watched by the stricken doers of the deed. They had
done all they could to make amends, having sent for a
gun and now were mounting guard to warn oncoming
cars. The poor mare, whose foal it was, ran backwards
and forwards, whinnying and squealing, wild eyed and
distracted, the most pitiful of all. She haunted the roadside for over a week, restless and still seeking the foal.

For something under a mile two of us at least walk with
our hearts in our mouths, Mr. Bundy ridden by the nightmare memory of the day when a fat man in a small car
ran over him and cut his head badly. Bill ambles along
still wearing his brainless smile, paying only the barest
attention to my feverish rating. He will never learn to
respect traffic although he has been run into by two motor
cycles, one car, and has sent three pedal cyclists flying.

But for this preoccupation I should be enjoying the
distant glimpses of the Isle of Wight's downs, showing
above Ridley Wood and Berry Beeches which lies on my
left across Ridley Plain, memorable as the place where I
saw two little stallions engaged in vigorous conflict. They
reared up, biting crest or foreleg, whichever came handy,
would fall to their knees, baffled, to fight better on
arising. The mares grazed calmly and unmoved, apparently indifferent to whom the victory fell.

None too soon comes the track we're looking for, running down over the heath and gorse-covered Marrowbones
Hill, past the fine holly clump where once the grey and
brown patched tepees of the gypsies used to look so lovely
against silver stem and shining dark green leaf; then

skirting Linford Enclosure and crossing another trickling streamlet it comes out at Linford.

Linford has a green with geese, ponies, and cattle, a small farm, and a big Sanatorium perched on top of the hill facing us. To the right is the little green valley lying between the two Linford Enclosures and crossed at the top by the meeting of Pinnick and Redshoot. It is cut down the middle by the wavering course of the Linbrook, weaving its way under thorns and gravel banks on its journey down to the Avon.

There are three good ways back from Linford to Ringwood. One is to follow the tarmac road uphill, taking the first turning on the right and keeping to it on its way round a handsome pine-clad hill, down past a farm, across the Moyles Court road, along the straight gravel road which ends abruptly among the bungalows, pigsties, and hen-runs which are the northern outskirts of Ringwood.

Another is to climb up past the Sanatorium and follow the gravel road through all its windings past woods and alongside the reappeared Linbrook until it joins the Moyles Court road by some almshouses. Here over the stile before us is the stream-following field-path we left on our right at the outset.

Third and last, turn right at the first left-hand bend the gravel road takes after passing the Sanatorium and climb any of the tracks running up the slope in front, for they all lead up to Rockford Common and into the main track.

CHAPTER II

IBSLEY, LINWOOD, AND HOME AGAIN

We began by exploring the north part of the Forest, and although Fritham is undoubtedly the best headquarters for operations in the north there are two more walks to be described from the angle of Ringwood before Fritham becomes our starting point, because, after consultation, we have decided to set down our walks in their order of discovery.

We had looked longingly from Rockford Common on many occasions at the neighbouring heights of Ibsley Common with its handsome clump of pines. We had developed a fondness for Whitefield Plantation because it had served us in such good stead as a landmark and was so shapely and dignified. ' One day,' we said to ourselves, ' we will climb those slopes and go and call on Whitefield Plantation.' But every time we set out across Rockford with this end in view we found the lure of the woods, Roe, Appleslade, Redshoot, and Milkham, irresistible and always ended up among their verdurous glooms and shadows numberless, avoiding each others' eyes on the way home.

In the end we decided that the only way to get closer acquainted with the pines was to flee temptation and go by road to Ibsley and down the lane that leads by Mockbeggar up to Ibsley Common.

The Salisbury road is good walking for human beings provided they go in single file, and for well-disciplined dogs who keep religiously to heel. As we walk in an undisciplined fashion we decided to do the two and a half miles by bus, a proceeding trying to Mr. Bundy who hates all petrol propelled vehicles.

14

FLIES AND SOME ANTIDOTES

We chose a cold and frosty morning for the expedition, the kind of day we prefer above all others for walking. Frost, though it keeps in the hounds, puts a spur in the air, drives the wild things out into the open, and kills the flies. Much as we love the Forest we must admit it has flies, for we should be doing our reader a bad turn if we allowed him to go unarmed against the stinging bandits into the glades and bottoms they frequent. Protective measures vary according to taste. Cigarette smoke saves some people, a mixture of one-part pennyroyal to three-parts sweet oil is strong enough to keep even horses safe for an hour if well smeared with it; I prefer citronel on handkerchief, forehead, wrists, and ankles. Bill and Mr. Bundy bite back, returning any victims in a most unbecoming and noisy way.

I know a charming lady who because she did not take any precautions against its flies, never hears the New Forest mentioned without a shudder. She began her honeymoon here, and returned to their cottage after the first rapt stroll in its solitudes with her young husband a changed woman. One eye was closed, her lip was swollen abominably, and her slim ankles now resembled pollard willows. Her tears were only staunched when she was shown the telegram announcing that a sea-coast hotel was eagerly waiting to receive them next day, for she felt that no man's heart could be proof against any further alterations of this kind in the face and figure of his beloved.

A kindly conductor helped us on to the ten o'clock bus to Salisbury, receiving Bill with undisguised admiration and bestowing upon Mr. Bundy's be-whiskered countenance an incredulous grin. He assisted us to dismount at Ibsley with even greater tenderness, having learnt by the way that all the scars on Bill's muzzle were due to rats of vast proportions and legendary ferocity, and that if Mr. Bundy's nose for scent were backed by a whippet's turn of speed our larder would be uncomfortably overcrowded with rabbits.

At Ibsley the Avon comes close against the road. It is spanned by a stone bridge of three arches leading to Harbridge; it has a noisy weir, and tall trees grow upon islands only big enough to allow them foothold above the water; often, too, there are wild-duck. Once, on a grey day, we were standing on the bridge looking down at the water when overhead a sound like goblin mouth-organs made us look up. Oh! splendid sight. Eight swans, their long necks stretched out before like Viking ships, their great wings beating in tune, swept by snowy against the dark clouds, as if the pages of Hans Andersen had fallen open and let the bewitched princes and their friends escape.

Rude things used to be said about the church that once stood at Ibsley. It was so neglected and damp that one wit said its walls were considered the sweetest pasture for sheep in this part of the land. It was replaced in the eighteenth century by a dull little building. Yet I seldom pass it without going in, for it holds an enchantingly comic monument to Sir John Constable.

Sir John, who was Francis Bacon's brother-in-law and had the honour of being the dedicatee of the 1612 edition of the *Essays*, is here shown kneeling with his wife at the foot of a spreading vine. This miraculous plant is laden

16

DOCKENSWATER, AT MOYLES COURT

not only with the purple clusters of its legitimate fruit but also bears the portraits of the Constable offspring, whose gloomy countenances peer out from among the leaves in a most resentful manner.

The lane by the church heads past cottages and small farms straight for Mockbeggar and the Ibsley uplands.

The sun was shining and the frost, hardening hoof-mark and wheel-rut to iron, had turned the grass margins white and furred the straws caught in brambles or dropped in the road. Birds puffed to twice their ordinary size hopped and ruffled it along the ditches, and the cows grouped at the field gates stood in misty clouds of their own breath.

At the meeting of our lane with the Moyles Court road occurred the only blot on an otherwise perfect day.

Bill, on the lead because we were not sure if he would be welcomed in the coverts beyond the fences, was attacked and badly bitten on his bland face by a low-minded, rough-haired tyke with a black eye. Roaring like a lion the indignant fellow fell upon his assailant; tearing the leash out of my hand and bearing him to the ground. Bill is by nature a pacifist. Like Harold Skimpole (ennobled by honour, of course) he only wishes to be allowed to live. As a result, having got the tyke at his mercy, his lack of experience so held him up that he had covered the poor wretch with dribblings born of much puffing and snarling before he finally seized it by the nose and shook it as vigorously as our energetic maid shakes her duster.

I rescued the offender, who fled howling, and turning beheld its jovial, red-faced master, bill-hook in hand, beaming at me over the fence. Before I could apologise for Bill's not turning his other cheek the old man cried delightedly, ' Shook un up prarper, didn't 'en ? Sarve 'en dam' well right ! '

Feeling rather weak about the knees I joined the dogs who were already half-way up the now rising gravel road. The keen air coming down from the Common soon blew all thought of the encounter from our minds and I was able to notice how the elms remained in the valley while the oaks followed the fences to the very foot of Common's bluffs, a few dying by the way and standing out bleached and stark against the twiggy darkness of their living comrades.

Straight up from the last little fence rise the first bluffs of the Common. Bracken begins and gorse, and in a stride or two the road is jostled by low hills thick in heather. The lonely house on the right was the home of the artist Maxwell Armfield, whose coloured wood engravings have often made me wish I was able to collect them.

Bill, his mind full of fur and feather, had rushed up the track and was out of sight when Mr. Bundy made the discovery of his life. In a disused gravel pit he found the graveyard of several ancient cars and motor-bikes and ran eagerly in and out among their mangled remains delighting in their downfall. When he came to my whistle, I had paused to indulge him, he was fairly dancing with triumph.

It was a charming experience to greet our dear acquaintances Rockford, with his cuckoo pines, Roe and Linford peering over his shoulder, from the long desired plateau. The views of even more purple moorlands and unknown woods to our left and ahead, too, filled us with exhilaration at the thought of fresh fields to conquer. But Whitefield plantation was rather disappointing. Like most public people it lost a great deal on closer acquaintance. Approached from behind it loses its symmetry, appearing elongated, and with a gap at one end so large that it gives the impression of one big and one small clump of trees instead of a united community. However, the pines were still tall enough to dwarf the rough-coated ponies nibbling the furze in their shelter.

The track runs straight across the Common, leaving Whitefield on its right and for some way is boldly marked, but as it nears the far edge of the Common it dwindles to a tiny path almost hidden by the heather, and drops down to join a network of similar footpaths threading their way through Linwood bog.

The bog lies spread at the foot of the Common like a huge golden-brown bearskin rug, and beyond it are the rising woods of Linwood and the as yet hidden Dockens Water; on the left the big mass of Hasley, and on the right, just showing still, the tops of Milkham and Roe above some half-tamed hillside fields.

We descended into the bog, now strengthened by the frost, and bearing left soon got into a well-defined track filled with thick slabs of ice and frozen moss, and following it heard first the rippling hurry of a stream, and then, as it entered a few sound yards of turf, saw between stunted oaks a plank bridge under a low, dark pine. We rested

19

on the bridge, watching the ale-coloured water pushing swiftly past its frozen edges and diving and wriggling through its ice-coated timber breakwater. Trees tilt across it, furze and brambles grow on its bank, hiding kingfisher and heron, and throwing dusky shadows on the surface where little trout still lurk and where once the proud salmon came to spawn, finding the gravelly depths perfect for nurseries. Alas! they no longer come, and the reason for their neglect stands at Fritham still though it is powerless to harm now. The powder mills built near the village a long while ago so tainted the water that cattle refused to drink it, and the fish holding their noses fled, never, in the case of the salmon, to return.

Before going ahead we turned about to take another look at the purple-brown slopes of the Common rising above the fawns and umbers of the bog, at the white cutting low down on one hillside, at the little pines on Black Barrow, and looming, colourful Hasley.

In the grey sand of the track we followed right-handed over the humpy, heathy bit before us Jack Frost had set hard the moulds of hound-pad and delicate, grooved shoe. He had also held firmly to the ground a bright silk hand-herchief which I stuffed into my pocket as a memento of this brilliant morning.

The track, nodding goodbye to the wasteland, goes between neat hedges and becomes a respectable, unadventurous and pretty gravel lane, crossed by an occasional runnel and leading past mud-walled thatched cottage and small farm up into Linwood where it joins the road that crosses Broomy and Ocknell Plains.

Opposite, Appleslade Enclosure dips and climbs. It is only a small wood of no particular beauty, but its name is said to mean Apple Valley (slade means valley in the Forest), and children gather sweet chestnuts here in good years, so it cannot be passed by without a word. Wild apple-trees are common still in the Forest, but Appleslade has none now.

We could have gone up through Appleslade, or up through the track skirting it on the right, but we preferred to turn right and following the road along for a while ascend to Rockford under the cuckoo pines. Bill was delighted, even though he had to be put on the lead till we left the road, because rabbits of most sporting qualities live all round the pines. I was glad, too, because we passed a farm with a streamlet running under its gate and an oak whose branches made shadow patterns on its barn's new thatch.

I have never seen Ibsley's slopes more lovely than they looked from Rockford that day. Dark heather, red bracken and bleached grass were so blended and mingled that they made me think of tortoiseshell. From under the cuckoo pines, lying in dazzling sun, they really were very beautiful. I stood and looked, listening to the drone of an airplane high overhead, until Mr. Bundy, always in a hurry, started busily prodding me with both fore-paws and blowing his elfin horn, unable to endure further delay.

Away then we went, right across Rockford, reminded by a distant shot in the green valley on our right of the farmer in leggings with gun, game-bag, and black labrador, we had seen on our way out, hoisting himself over a gateway at Ibsley in search of pigeon; down Bracken Hill, and up the lane that passes one of the many stiles of our field-path to Ringwood. In something under an hour the cuckoo pines were far away and I was seated opposite my mother, expatiating on the wonders of the new walk, and two bowls were being emptied with astonishing speed and ungentlemanly noises by my good companions on either side of the hearth.

The country we had seen lying north of Ibsley Common was so striking that we could not rest until we had gone to it. Fortunately for us the frost that had seized upon the land in a single night with the suddenness of an inspiration had become an *idée fixe* and paralysed it completely, holding up the seepings of the hillsides, putting backbone into the bogs and making the wettest tracks we knew hard and sound. But for this frosty blessing we should have waited till the summer before we trusted ourselves unguided in land where for all we knew there were no good tracks. No good tracks! But then we only knew Hampton Ridge as two dotted lines on the map running parallel from Frogham to Fritham.

We got Miss Riley out of the garage because we wanted to get to Frogham as soon as we could, and we did not want to walk about 18 miles, as we should have to do if we covered the Moyles Court road on foot as well as doing the run we had marked out for ourselves in the new country.

It was, as a Wiltshire labourer said to a parson friend of ours, weather to make you wait upon your nose. In other words the wind was icy, the sky a frozen grey, and the

Forest looked dark and forbidding. But it could not stop us, for we were hungry to make the new land ours. Even Miss Riley, who hates the cold and spat with fury at the outset because I had neglected the usual preliminary attentions she considers her due on arctic mornings, soon entered into our eager mood, and nobly battered her way through the frozen Linbrook where it crosses the road at North Poulner. Our thunderous crunchings made no impression on the fat pony on the opposite side of the splash whose master was waiting for us to break a passage for him through the ice.

We purred along the winding road past Bracken Hill and Three Tree Hill, the beginning and end of Rockford Common's southern boundary, and were glad to find Dockenswater still himself when we reached the Moyles Court cross-roads.

What a pretty meeting of the ways it is ! The finest oak in the district grows just above the stream on a green rise, and across the Linwood road mounts Three Tree Hill with its group of rugged pines, its purple heather, and its great creamy sandpit. Over the water stands Moyles Court itself, a sober red house backed by woods and neighboured by barns and stables.

I suppose nearly everyone knows the story of Moyles Court; but at the risk of resembling those anguishing people who, after prefacing a narrative with the prayer that we stop them if we know it, hold on doggedly in spite of our most ardent nods and becks, I must relate a local version.

A cunning, grasping fellow called Dunne, a native of

these parts, was greatly moved on hearing that rich rewards were to be had for giving information regarding the whereabouts of any fugitives from Sedgemoor. Some evil sprite put into his hands two such unfortunates. Anxious to have them in safe keeping while he went for the soldiers he racked his brains until they suggested as innocent gaoler Dame Alice Lisle of Moyles Court. He knew that, though a loyal subject of James herself, her large heart would not allow her to turn a hunted fellow-creature from her door. All went as he had hoped, and as soon as he had seen them safely bestowed he spurred away to Fordingbridge and fetched the troopers.

The result was that the first victim of the Bloody Assize was poor Dame Alice. Though three times acquitted by the jury she was executed in Winchester, at the age of seventy.

She lies in a plain stone table tomb with Agnes Harfell, her daughter, on the right of the porch in Ellingham churchyard. The church is old, tiny, charming, and reached by a good road running through trees for a mile behind the house. But for the risk of accidents happening to Bill in the coverts on either side of the road we should pay the church frequent visits, for it has a blue and gold triangular sundial over the porch, an ancient chancel screen with an hour-glass bracket, a carved Jacobean pulpit, the Lisles' canopied pew, and, set in some handsomely carved panelling that was once the reredos, a picture taken from Port St. Mary during Drake's famous raid on Cadiz Bay. The painting is a lurid Last Judgement; more muscular than beautiful, but I like it because I can imagine Mr.

24

Dunne as any one I wish of the screaming gentlemen being dragged into the Pit by the demons.

Miss Riley waded through Dockenswater and carried us smoothly along, refusing to stop in spite of Bill's entreaties as portly rabbits lolloped lazily away to right and left. The road goes pleasantly on, escorted by trees and fields on the one side and Ibsley Common's frontiers on the other, crosses the green at pretty South Gorley where we cast a respectful look up the lane which passes Mr. Sumner's house on Cuckoo Hill, and fords Latchmore Brook where it runs down fresh from the Forest uplands and its passage between Furze and Gorley Hills. Furze Hill has a topknot of seven trees called Gorley Firs which act as a landmark for a number of miles around. On still goes our road past North Gorley, as charming as her southern sister, and we went with it until, after four miles of nearly straight going, it forks and we, turning right, climbed up the hill to Hyde Common and crossing its open gorsey stretch arrived at last in Frogham.

It is curious how often people living close by a place know little or nothing about it. At the first cottage I stopped to ask the way to Hampton Ridge and the woman who came to the door was unable to tell me. Wrapping a shawl about her she came into the road with me and summoning a neighbour stated my difficulty. Both were kind and anxious to help, but neither could say more than that they'd heard of it and knew it to be somewhere hereabouts. They said the moor was thick in tracks and I could not hope to find the one I wanted among so many without help. Fortunately, just as I was returning to the car, where two anxious faces were peering through the windows, a labourer heavily burdened with moustaches came majestically along the road on a bicycle. At once all was smiles and nods of encouragement on the part of my two dear old dames, and their assurances that now it would be all right as Mr. Seymour, he knew about the moors, and had lived hereabouts even longer than they had, hindered the said Mr. Seymour from giving the desired information for quite an appreciable time.

With conscious pride Mr. Seymour waited till they ceased to prattle and then,

' Tarn right at that crarse-rods,' he said, ' goo past Farester's Arms and kip gooin' till the next crarse-rods and you'll see Hampton Ridge straight ahead. You can't mistake him.'

He was right, there was no possibility of mistaking that sporting ribbon which bleached by sun and wind sweeps down through moorland from Windmill Hill only to mount swiftly again up the high, heathered bluff, standing over 300 feet above sea-level, which is the beginning of the Ridge. On it runs straight as a die through some of the wildest, finest country we know in the north of the New Forest. To the right, line on line of dark, low hills come dipping and rolling down to Latchmoor Bottom and on that bleak day they seemed to float in the faint and frozen haze covering the land. Streamlets and pools, rigid in the bitter embrace of the frost, glittered like steel out of the dusky heather. Hasley looked stern and aloof, standing high on his hill between Latchmore Bottom and Dockenswater's rough little moorland vale, hidden from

26

us now. The woods ahead were brooding and mysterious, the moors and hills and trees of the Godshill and Ashley Walk country stood frowning on the left.

We scrambled out of Miss Riley, and by the time I had piled all our rugs upon her nose Bill was a white dot among the heather of the Ridge. The wind was of the kind that bids nor sit, nor stand, but go, so Mr. Bundy and I set off at a run and were soon panting up the side of the ridge. At the top the north-easter filled my eyes with tears at the first stinging encounter and made it impossible for me to park my handkerchief for the rest of the way. But I did not mind, for who could mind trifles with country, beautiful even when blurred by wind-born tears, lying all round, and with a good manly track to carry you high up through the heart of it?

The fat cats in the cottages at Frogham had made me suspect a quantity of ground game to come, and though I never saw any I knew it must be in every bush and hag, for Mr. Bundy's loyalty broke down before its scented lure, and after a few agitated, apologetic whimpers he was off like a shot. For the rest of the way until we reached Amberwood I watched his little brown body bobbing up and down in the heather and knew he was deaf and blind to all but the gamey smells around him.

Blackcock, as late as the first years of this century, were seen on these hills, and still I am told the lovely, melancholy whistle of the curlew is heard above them in the Spring. I hope one day to hear him here, for I have never forgotten the first time I heard him calling over the moors above Wensleydale where, for the first time, too,

27

I heard the snipe at his drumming. My father, with whom I went for splendid walks, not to be equalled now he is gone, was with me at the time. We thought we heard a lamb bleating and ran first to one side of the walled way up to the moors, then to the other, peering over them after the poor little lost creature, and much puzzled by the way in which its voice seemed to come now from here, now from there. It was quite by chance that he looked up and discovered the tiny drummer soaring and diving overhead.

We had meant to follow the track's left fork right round past Islands Thorns to Telegraph Hill, but we had reckoned without Amberwood.

A row of pines stand nobly along its crest and there is a cottage at its northern hatch gate, past which our track goes down through part of Islands Thorns and Amberwood and up to Fritham. Its slopes are covered thickly with oaks, hollies and thorns, and it is threaded by Latchmore Brook. It was planted in 1815, and in later years when some trees were being cleared for a nursery to be made in it, there were found hidden among their roots old broken pottery and some small hand-grindstones, once used by the British potters in Roman times who had their being here. It is, moreover, a favourite messuage of the deer, a herd of 15 bucks having been seen here by Mr. Sumner.

Knowing all this we found as soon as we reached it that we could not turn away from it and passed through the gate, only pausing to admire two giant tabbies entrenched behind the cottage gate before hurrying down the grassy ride descending the slope on our left. The dogs to my surprise never left the ride, nor did they desert me when I dawdled on the bridge over the brook.

The ride led us to another gate which opens on to a wide green track with Sloden Enclosure rising steeply on the other side. This track, had we turned left, would have taken us to Fritham, but we were for Latchmore Bottom and so went right, stepping over the trickles oozing out of Sloden Enclosure and taking advantage of the dry foothold afforded by the rushes when we came to soggy bits. Sheltered by trees on either hand and lying between two hills the track had hardly felt the frost at all and we should have done better had we waited until summer when it would have been drier going.

Here, too, both dogs kept to the track as they had to the ride, untempted by the gorgeous smells that must have been hanging about in the woods on either hand. Of course, it was absurd, but when I thought of the Roman-British dwellings in Amberwood and remembered that the sombre pines of Sloden Enclosure stood over a mass of ancient potteries, when I listened to the sullen whisperings of the pines and glanced into their eerie depths under that curdled sky, I did begin to wonder if hundreds of grimy, misty figures might not be scowling at us from behind the tree trunks.

I do not believe in ghosts, but all the most convincing, first-hand ghost stories told me by those who do, started to crop up in my mind. There were those monks seen by the practical young Scotswoman who was making her south country farm pay when everybody else was gazing hopelessly at the linings of their pockets. The land had belonged to the Knights Templars, who had left it on account of the plague. All that remains of their habitation of it are the now earth-covered surrounding wall and the small chapel and hospital combined. The present farmhouse was built long after the knights had left. My Scots friend has a clever daughter who was acquiring much distinction at an agricultural college when I paid her a visit, and this girl had for her bedroom the long room under the roof. One night she woke up suddenly to find sitting on the foot of her bed, and wearing a monk's garments, a distinguished looking man with a short, pointed, grey beard. He nodded to her smilingly and vanished.

The room now lost its attractions for the young lady, who much amused her mother by refusing to sleep there again. The maternal amusement was short-lived. One afternoon in winter my friend went to her own room and saw occupying the middle of it two monks engaged in conversation. They turned as she came in, and looking at her quietly and slowly faded away, but not before she had recognised in one of them her daughter's grey-bearded friend. The other was short and a cripple. Not long after this meeting the plough, at work in what was once the monks' graveyard, brought to the surface the skeleton of a little man with hip disease. All this she told me herself, and then added the nastiest bit of all. She went on a visit to Scotland to stay with an old friend who was superstitious enough to wish to visit a crystal-gazer. They went, but after peering some time into her crystal the 'gazeuse' said, 'I can tell you nothing. Your friend is

a disturbing influence and she is surrounded by monks.'
Horrid to walk into a ghost in a haunted house, but hor-
rider still to think that when you walk out of it he may
come with you !

And then I thought of the little old lady in black who
still potters happily about the house in Winchester she
should have left two or three hundred years ago ; and
of the house in Ireland belonging to a friend of mine,
whose iron knocker's unaided thunderings mean death or
accident to whoever opens the door in response ; and of
the beautiful girl in the brocade dress who walked in
broad daylight on a tèrrace I know of but have promised
not to name, nor to relate the details of the story and the
reason for her appearance.

Though the sun now broke through the clouds and lit
up the sage green trunks of Amberwood's oaks it only
made the Sloden Enclosure pines more black and stark,
and when the oaks gave way to more pines as Amberwood
melted into Alderhill Enclosure, and the murmurings
grew louder and louder, we felt that the trees were crowd-
ing vengefully in on us though the track remained as wide
as ever and we nearly took ignominiously to our heels.

It was with a sigh of relief that we noted the gradual
thinning of the pines and saw at last through their boles
the hills of the honest moorland beyond. The ground
grew sounder, the turf shorter, and though a few young
pines, escaped from the Enclosures, stood across the track
as though to bar our way we were soon out in the open
again.

Under the sun all looked genial. The hills appeared

31

glad to see us, Hasley looming on the left looked kindly on us, and the wide green stretch of Latchmore Bottom beckoned us quite openly.

The track runs on through the Bottom, which is studded with hollies, thorns, and a scattering of seedling pines. As we gained it a sharp little angry voice from one of the pinelets made me glance to the left. A wren was scolding us from its twigs, bobbing about in great rage. It followed us for a pinelet or two, and then with a final vindictive trill buzzed away back into the gloomy depths of the pinewoods. Was it an envoy from the potteries ? Mr. Bundy does not scout the idea. We did not ask Bill as he was far away on the hills again, nor have we ever told him about it as we did not want to worry him, he suffers so from nightmare, poor fellow.

The brook hardly lowered its voice the whole way along and kept close to the track. Above it on the right we saw against the darkness of a clump of hollies some crimson rags drying on the bushes and then the tents, some grey, some ironstone-coloured, and one vivid emerald green, of the gypsies encamped there. This rise, I learned from a pleasant young forester, is called Marrowbones Hill. He had never heard of the other Marrowbones Hill above Linford Enclosure where there used to be another gypsy *pied-à-terre*. He told me quite a lot about the country, and from him I learned that Rockford and Ibsley Common aren't in the New Forest at all legally. Though to the walker this information is of no account, for there is nothing to show where the Forest stops and the common lands begin, it is of great importance to the man who lives

32

STREAM FISHED BY HERONS

on the commons, for the common rights are more worth having than those of the Forest, where he must pay a grazing fee, collected by the agistors, for his ponies, cows, and pigs, and only gets free a certain number of turfs and cords of wood. On the common, though he may neither shoot nor fish, he may graze his cattle as freely as he may take gravel, sand, turf, furze, fern, and heather sufficient for his own use.

We joined a gravel road at Ogdens, a small farm at the end of the Bottom, and crossing the brook climbed the slope on our right, not realising till we reached the top and saw Miss Riley's brown back that we were back on Windmill Hill again.

CHAPTER III

WITH FRITHAM FOR BASE OR HASLEY, MOOR-LAND, OLD SLODEN AND BROOMY ENCLO-SURE

FRITHAM, high on the hills, commands the whole of the north of the Forest, and as it is charming and retired, receiving motor-cars but rarely, it is the best possible place for a walker to stay. The only trouble is that the tiny inn prefers only one guest, and not a great many of the cottagers are prepared to take visitors. Those among them who are may be found by enquiry at the post-office or at the ' Royal Oak.'

On every side but one the woods lie within call, not thinly populated enclosures hardly bigger than copses but fine deep communities of trees in which long hours can be spent. On the village green oaks and hollies grow quite thickly, affording shelter to lazy white pigs and to geese who, with the dignity of an elderly gentleman on a tricycle, trundle away at the approach of the stranger. There are one or two houses, a school, some colour-washed thatched cottages, and trim and inviting under a tree the ' Royal Oak,' which gives its name to one of the meets most popular with the buckhounds, deer abounding in the neighbouring woods.

The green is cut by three tracks running fanwise into the hollies, a fourth skirting it goes down the hill on the left. The ' Royal Oak ' stands at their meeting with the road which comes down and up again from the plains between Stony Cross and Brook.

It was a sunny morning early in Spring when we took our first walk from Fritham. Choosing the middle of the three tracks across the green we went under the hollies and oaks for a few yards, and then, as the track began to

36

descend, found ourselves out on an open hillside where an army of hollies with an occasional oak for sentry bivouacked on the slopes to right and left. Below us and clothing the opposing hillside were the close-packed tree-tops of Islands Thorns and Amberwood, the impressive line of the latter's pines topping the hill. To the left of these woods the pines, oaks and ashes of Sloden Enclosure came trooping down, while on the right, beyond some grass fields where several horses grazed, the red walls and slate roofs of a few cottages showed up grouped round a big white building.

This group we knew was the relict of the powder factory whose labours had driven the salmon from the little brooks below forever. A cart hauled by a stocky little horse appeared toiling up our track, and so we took the opportunity of asking the man in attendance if the white building were the factory. He said that it had been the factory's stables and had held the forty or fifty horses used for carrying the powder away.

As the track ran on the slopes on either hand kept revealing new charms, chief among them the enchanting views of the long pond called Irons Well, which lies near the powder works. I first saw its intensely blue oval through a group of hollies and oaks growing close against the track. Woods just brushed with young green stood about it and grass slipped smoothly down to its margin. The powder factory being hidden by the trees might not have been there, and the pond seen from afar across the rough hillside looked as secret and serene as a dryad's bathing pool. It kept hiding and reappearing as we

37

continued our descent, different each time we saw it and perhaps loveliest when the blue gave way to reflected trees and a swan moving majestically showed suddenly against the shadows of its far bank.

Swans as a rule have the same effect upon me as rhododendrons, Shetland ponies, and prize collie dogs. They seldom look as though they belong to their country surroundings, and they remind me of that dreadful photogravure family whose grouped portraits were so popular in Edwardian nurseries. A gorgeous Georgian gentleman and his baby-faced spouse are the parents, the children are impossibly pretty little girls in satin slippers and long frocks and cherubic small boys in velvet suits and ringlets. They spend their time feeding swans or ' romping ' with a collie dog or a Shetland pony in an atmosphere of long grass, marble steps and wreathed smiles.

But this swan took its place at once with the two other swan memories I cherish—the flight of eight over Ibsley Bridge and the tragic pair I saw on the Avon one day. They kept close together, and to my great surprise let me get right up to them without making any effort to evade me though they saw me quite well on the treeless marge. When level with them I saw that the wings and flank of one were crimsoned with blood stains, and realised that his mate was too loyal to leave him even at the approach of a human being.

The nearer the woods we got the sturdier and more numerous became the oaks, and we saw two of them had each adopted a small yew, letting it grow up under their branches. Probably the yews were seeded waifs from

38

Old Sloden. Bill and Mr. Bundy were having a glorious time in the rough on either side of the track, and became delirious with expectancy when we entered the woods through the hatch standing across the track at the bottom of the hill.

The track is an excellent one. Dry and sound and made of gravel it runs all the way from Fritham, up through Amberwood, and on to Hampton Ridge without once changing its nature. For its entire length of about four miles, from Fritham to Frogham, it never once touches dull or ugly country.

On first entering the woods it invades the southern edge of Islands Thorns, and then, bending left-handed, passes through another gate and enters Amberwood. All the way tall and slender oaks grow as close together as their branches will allow, and the sunlight is only splashed about their grey-green trunks and on the grass and brambles below in narrow streaks and tiny pools. The voice of Latchmore brook made itself heard above the various bird arias and recitatives quite soon after we entered Islands Thorns, and shortly the track crossed it where, wide and shallow, it comes winding along through the trees, having filled Irons Well to the brim on its way down from the hills.

The track lingers in the woods, bending about as though it were trying to stay with the trees as long as possible. On its way it passes through another gate and shortly afterwards goes steeply up Amberwood's hill, just skirting the rails. Firs and oaks, together with hollies stout and twisted of trunk, are thick on the right, and among them

39

near the top of the hill is a low-growing oak covered with huge crusty blains as to trunk and bearing a host of ferns upon its branches.

At the top of the hill a fleet of pursy cats—tabby, tortoiseshell, and one delightful grey-and-white fellow—streamed from the bushes into Amberwood Cottage's garden, while hysterical hens rose squawking in a cloud as Bill cantered past. It is typical of his good understanding that he is now quite trustworthy with fowls. When he first came to us we had much ado to rescue from his jaws an idiot Leghorn that had flown off a nest-box into his face and of which he had, with the instinct of the epicure, seized a wing.

Wakey, our dear and handsome maid, and I had removed him with difficulty, and being whipless had spanked him with a horse-radish leaf! From that day to this he has never ' back-slidden,' and, moreover, helps to shepherd back to the run any strayed bird.

Though Amberwood's sunlit recesses looked alluring over the gate we kept on with the track and were soon out in the open country of the Ridge, walking as if on air. The Dorset highlands ahead, the moorland's hills, vales, and woods on our right, the ridges and woodlands across Latchmore Bottom, cut by its brook's gleaming curves and watched over by Hasley, were all radiant under the Spring sun. The breeze, evidently full of provocative messages for the dogs, as both had deserted me, brought intoxicating odours .to me of green heather, of warm moist soil, of streams, of pinewoods. It was a grand day, with Hasley's heart for its goal.

The Linwood Road to Fritham

Turning left on Windmill Hill we crossed the brook, Mr. Bundy and Bill bathing and gulping in passing, and worked our way by irregular tracks over the tumbled heath to the western gate of Hasley.

It was a great moment when we first peered over that gate and up the green ride, which, impatient to reach the summit of the hill, soars up at a prodigious gradient, cutting its way through the trees with a fine scorn for the zig-zagging which a less ardent climber would have considered more restful. We had seen the wooded hill so often and from so many points of vantage, and on every occasion it had looked so masterful that we were amazed on finding its interior as gentle as the dove. Here were not only bleak pines but kindly oak and sweet chestnut, the latter showering the ride with its canoe-shaped leaves, and masses of bluebells and hosts of primroses. If the moorland scents were delicious the breath of Hasley was ravishing. Smells mean a lot to us three, though our tastes differ widely. Things long dead appeal to Mr. Bundy, and game scents and food scents stand high in Bill's mind. I love the smell of new bread on a frosty morning, of horses warm from their work, of corn rooms, of wood fires, and new leather, and new books, and some kinds of furniture polish, and grass mowings, and applelofts, and milk as it flows warm from the udder and mingles with the kind pastureland smell clinging to the cow's coat, and frosty evenings in London, and many, many more too numerous to tell. But this bouquet offered by Hasley seemed at the time to roll them all over. What could be more lovely than the blend of bluebell, primrose, and pine? I doubt if even the Dorset nosegay whose fragrance up till then I had considered supreme (gorse-bloom, sea, and hay it was) could beat it.

I knew Bill, too, would find the rank odours he loves here, because foxes and deer frequent the wood, and he soon proved me right by disappearing, accompanied by crackings of dead twigs and tearing of brambles. There was nothing to tickle the palate of Mr. Bundy, mercifully.

Hasley hill was planted with trees in 1846, and before that I suppose was as bare and heathery as the Ridge itself. Mr. Sumner thinks that possibly the Sloden potters delved here for the fire-resisting ironstone they used in their kilns, because there are old diggings on the north-eastern side of the hill and the soil is stained by iron as red as the foxes who inhabit here.

Having gone up with a run the track gets its climbing over quickly, goes smoothly for a bit, and then descends as soon as the end of the wood comes into sight. Out through the gate it goes and disappears at once, leaving us to find our way as best we might across what at first appeared to be a pathless, undulating, waste of heather. About three-quarters of a mile ahead, rising nobly above the moors and streaked by a broad white track, was the hill that bears Old Sloden upon its back, so I knew we should stumble soon upon our end of that track if we had a bit of luck to start with.

In our short experience of the Forest we have learned to distrust all but the boldest tracks, as so many footpaths which began quite confidently had, after much meandering, become weak-minded and dithered away altogether, leaving us either in a bog or by some old turf-cutting scars. But this time luck was with us, for we chose the right hand one of two narrow paths just showing through the heather and were almost immediately dropped into the hither end of the track we wanted. Soon we were climbing up the hillside and thinking how pleasant Latchmore Bottom looked from these new moors and how nice it was to have recognised the bright, bush-hung ensigns of the gypsies on Marrowbones Hill. Then we came in among the oaks, ashes, and thorns, the whitebeams, hollies, and crab-apple trees which make Old Sloden so varied and so beautiful. The yews are very numerous here, and I was glad, because I love their fluted stems and their dark, dense leafage which looks more than ever mysterious against the tender transparence of the young green opening on their neighbours' branches.

The track turns to grass under the trees and runs straight ahead and close to the bank which once carried the fence of potter-haunted Sloden Enclosure. To Mr. Bundy I owe my first kiln discovery, or rather the discovery of where a kiln had been. I went with him to a rabbit hole he was interested in, and saw, mixed in the black earth, a lot of broken, grey earthenware. Though no antiquary I confess I was really thrilled by our find and picked up a sherd or two, rather awed by the thought that the last human hand to touch it had fallen into dust more than 1000 years ago.

In Old Sloden is a square earthwork believed to have walled in a potter settlement, but even this information

43

and the further knowledge that the mystic symbol of the Druids grows on the more north-westerly of the white-beams, did not make us feel potter-watched that day. In fact we fell as much in love with Old Sloden as we had been scared by his neighbour and namesake within whose boundary we had found our kiln's remains, deciding that he was a jovial old fellow and well deserving the honour of being considered the most beautiful hillside wood in the north of the Forest.

Too soon we were out on the rough heath which runs for about a mile between Old Sloden and Fritham. Leaving our grass track we joined the stony one running from Fritham down through Sloden across Latchmore brook and into Holly Hatch. Us it took pleasantly back to Fritham, where, as we had expected, it turned out to be the left of three which cross the green.

Our next walk taken from Fritham was taken under a cloudless summer sky and a blazing sun. The day is marked in our memories with a red letter in the largest type.

Lured on by the thought of Old Sloden we set out along the middle track, leaving it when we reached the trees and picking up the grass track on our right easily enough at first because Sloden Enclosure's bank and gateless posts showed us where to go. As we advanced it began to look perplexing, as all new roads do when seen from the opposite end for the first time. We had not noticed that there were two places where it forked, and it was fortunate that we decided to take the right-hand track at the first fork and to bear left at the second where an oak stands, drooping its branches so low that to avoid stooping one goes round them.

I think the best place to see for the first time the moor between Hasley and the Slodens is from the brow of Old Sloden's hill, in the shade of his yews, on a hot summer day. They lie in the sun so blissfully, flowing away with a gentle dip and swell, sometimes hiding sometimes revealing the white track that leads to Hasley shimmering and dreamy in the distance, and all around them are woods dim in the heat haze, and far away behind Hasley sleep the opalescent hills of Dorset.

Out of the wood the sun gave no quarter, baking the sand and gravel of the track to such a temperature that poor Mr. Bundy took to the heather, preferring the extra exertion of popping up and down all the way to Hasley to burning his pads on the pebbles. It is curious how white the pebbly tracks look, because on close acquaintance the stones prove to be all different colours—grey, blue, copper, and yellow.

Hasley's cool was grateful after the moorland heat and we were sorry to leave it, and, turning left, to take a track apparently used by water far more often than by man or beast. It always seems to be in a mess, and its soft, boggy bits plentifully bespatter Bill's white jacket and my stockings every time we use it.

It negotiates Ogden's Purlieu, a pleasant, unkempt heathland sown with young pines and lying in the circle made by Hasley, Ibsley Common, Linwood, and Broomy Enclosure. Dockenswater, descending from the hills through south Bentley Wood, trails across it, skirting Anses, Holly Hatch and Broomy Enclosure on its way.

Opposite the plank bridge which crosses the stream near where the track goes through it are one or two houses, and the gravel road which, leaving the moorland road by Milkham Enclosure, runs down past Ogden's Purlieu and rejoins the moorland road at Linwood.

We went left over the brook and headed for Broomy Enclosure. It is a bewitching wood and was in the pleasantest mood that day. Brightly painted, tiny flowers were generously sprinkled about the short grass of the ride; the oaks, tall and freely spaced, made the sun a welcome guest, their leaves tactfully preventing him from becoming too much for their other friends, and he in return made brilliant designs all over their green carpet.

Mr. Bundy titupped back and forth happily before me, birds whistled and winged it among the branches, and across the ride zoomed an occasional bee; there were no flies. All was peace. Bill was cantering easily a few yards away with no more than his usual look of hopeful expectancy, and I was thinking how wise Michael Angelo had been to go to the wood-hung mountains of Spoleto for comfort after old Urbino's death, for, as he said of them, ' truly there is no peace save in the woods,' when the trees on the right unexpectedly backed away and formed a half circle about a hillock rough with bracken and brambles, and few self-sown young trees. Bill had just began bouncing in the heather at its base when he suddenly flung himself forward. There was a crackling, a rustle, a sharp thud, and up, out and away,

46

with Bill flying a milky streak close to its heels, bounded our first deer.

Up the curve of the knoll she went, rapping the hollow-sounding ground with her hard little hoofs, at each lengthening leap flipping her legs close to her golden-brown body, ears cocked forward, head stretched towards the trees, snowy tail spread like a tiny triangular sail. It was a lovely sight to watch them race away over the curve of the hill and it was unspoilt by any fear that the flight would end in terror and blood.

Bill, excited as never before, tore along uttering a string of half-strangled falsetto yappings entirely out of keeping with his bulk and displaying a turn of speed I never dreamt he possessed. In fact, I was so bedazzled by the beauty of the spectacle, and amazed by Bill's display, that it was not until the trees had swallowed them up that I thought of my duty and started calling Bill in every key expressive of command, rage, entreaty, and endearment. It seemed impossible that the woods could be so silent with those two careering through them so madly; not a sound of the chase was to be heard. At last he came back. Not white any more, nor tidy, but gasping for breath, covered with blood, and torn all over by the brambles he had charged through. The blood being his own I regained my calm, rated him, slapped him with his collar (I had suffered much, expecting to hear the shot that would spell his passing), but he didn't care. He had had a royal time and I could not take it from him.

Completely happy, his stern high, he trotted along the ride ahead and was soon gambolling foolishly about a

47

bashful cocker spaniel maiden.   She lives in the cottage by the gate opening on to the gravel track which goes over Latchmore brook, up through Old Sloden and across the heath to Fritham.

CHAPTER IV

EYEWORTH, ISLANDS
THORNS AND THE RIDGE

D

OUR most memorable walk from Fritham was taken in one of the earliest months of the year on a still sunny morning, which set the moist land twinkling all over. Every runnel, every stream was on the move again after a week or more of the repose forced upon them by a record frost. The birds were in such good voice, the air so warm, the breeze so gentle that it was more like April than mid February.

That the sweetness of the morning had drawn all the householders of brake and branch into the open was made patent by the antics of the dogs. Bill was racing about in the conviction that this morning he was certain to find something to give him a good hunt; Mr. Bundy was so excited that he executed a farandole as he went on ahead of me and accompanied it by a song composed by himself, containing some notes so piercing that they would put a slate pencil skating over its native slate to shame. Their good spirits were infectious, making me feel I wanted to imitate Mr. Bundy and dance down the hill, a desire I should probably have given way to but for the young man coming up the track with a posse of heifers. For we had not only the bright morning to excite us; we were bound for Eyeworth, Islands Thorns, and the moors about them.

To do this we had to pass Irons Well, so we took the right-hand track across the green. From the first, through the hollies standing up stoutly all over the grassy hillside, we had the lovely pool to look at, its swan upon its breast, its lawns and trees reflecting themselves in every part of the water not occupied already by the sky. The closer we got to it the more delectable it appeared. The rushing and splashing noise that floated up the hill to greet us had prepared us for the waterfall down whose stone steps Latchmore brook escapes into the woods ; but of the tiny islets growing up out of the water no hint was given. They are tufted with absurd little trees, and must, we are sure, be tenanted by the more select, the *élite*, of the water society folk.

It is all so charming that really the powder factory buildings do not matter in the least. You just turn your back on them, your feet at the pond's lip, and gaze contentedly across the water at the trees rising on every side, at the mist of bushes closing the far end, and at the golden road running past on the right. This road we recognised was one to be followed, and decided to explore it as soon as we could. This morning we wanted to spend our time in the woods.

The swan was evidently used to being fed, for he came swimming up to us, an expectant look in his eye. At his approach Bill started to play the idiot, pretending to be afflicted with a consuming thirst which the water within a few feet of the majestic bird alone could quench. The swan took an instant dislike to the impertinent animal and bore down upon him hissing, whereupon he darted off in a half circle, only to enter the water again a little farther off. Unfortunately for the swan's dignity his rather elastic-side-boot looking legs, paddling furiously, were plainly visible through the clear water. In spite of his comic appearance I knew it might go hard with Bill if he caught the dog, for who has not heard the awe-inspiring stories of the damage done by swans to wrongdoers found in the vicinity of the nest? Our old nanny said she knew of a man whose leg was broken by one blow of an angry swan's wing; she also told us how an egg-sucking retriever was caught robbing a swan's nest and was drowned by the male bird, who accomplished the feat by delivering blow after blow on the dog's head with his beak and beating the water with his wings, so that the unhappy animal was both blinded and choked by it.

With this in mind, and not approving of the baiting of the pool's lord, I bade Bill pull himself together, and leaving the bank we crossed over the bridge spanning the waterfall and entered Eyeworth by a ride on the right.

Eyeworth is a fine old wood, full of queer twisted trees with such oddities of growth that they make one think how much Arthur Rackham would love to meet them, and then wonder if, perhaps, he already has their acquaintance. They lean, they bend, they sport a gouty branch whose weight drags it to the ground, or from a bulge at their base they grow a family of straight saplings belonging to another breed altogether. The hollies in this wood cease to be stocky trees and here become tall, spindly bushes with lackadaisical branches trailing limply down and resembling the lianes of a tropical forest.

Very soon, however, the ride widens and takes on a splendid dignity as the beeches begin. Noble trunks, swathed in green moss at their beginning, turn to silver as they near the sky and spread out their branches in the sun. The ground is ruddy with their leaves and green at the ride's edge with a beautiful moss ; the same, I suppose, as that which, patterned with branch shadows, covers the tree trunks ; on the ground it develops big fern-like fronds.

At the time of the Domesday Survey the wood was called Ivare, a name meaning a wooded hill. It is a pity that now we misspell it, and odd that it ever came to be spelt Eyeworth at all, because the Forest people pronounce it ' Iver ' to this day. Islands Thorns, said to be a corruption of Highlands Thorns, and Studley Wood blend with Eyeworth so completely that to us the three of them are as one big wood, but to the Forest authorities each is quite a separate entity.

The ride we followed leaves the trees at the meeting of Eyeworth and Studley. On the right and standing back a little we saw an extra fine beech and took her to be Eyeworth's Queen, having read that her majesty inhabits the borders of the two woods.

Out of the wood, not knowing what the day held in store for us, we were content to pause, and drinking in the sunny, peaty air, to let our eyes wander over the valleys and hills, filled or topped by woods, that reached out before us. Had we known what we might have missed by lingering too long we would not have spared the view a second. As it was we idled away several minutes before we turned into the track, and followed it in all its leftward leanings till it brought us to the top of the dip in the moor, where, among heather, gorse, and hollies, one of the headsprings of Latchmoor Brook is born. Looking down on it we felt ' tickled at our hërtes rootes ' to think we had

53

found the fountain from which Fritham's lovely pool had sprung, and the beginning of the stream we had grown so familiar with in its woodland and moorland stages. It was, we considered, an amusing thought that a stream is the only thing in existence whose childhood is everlasting, however big it may grow. Though we may first see it in its old age, so city-weary and so burdened with the cares of commerce that it is thankfully losing itself in the invulnerable sea, yet we know we have only to go back along its banks a little way to find it at lusty manhood among the thriving country towns it has brought into existence ; in graceful adolescence idling through meadows and under leaning willows ; as a child, playing with its coloured pebbles and the thyme and forget-me-nots on its inch-high banks ; and, at last, fresh from the cold womb of the earth, bubbling delightedly to itself in its cradle on some high chalk down or lonely moor. Having waxed so heroic about rivers in general we felt almost aggrieved that Latchmoor brook never grows out of its childish ways, nor attains to the ocean, but is content to drop into the Avon when still at the nursery stage.

Because we were so absorbed by the spring we did not give the opposite slope a glance for several minutes, and when we did the first thing that struck us was the marvellous contrast made by the light trunks of a few scattered beeches against the dark hollies and heather. Particularly lovely was the group of these trees on the verge of Studley. The hill slants so steeply that it looked to us as if the leaf-covered ground touched their branches. Suddenly there was a white flicker under the beeches, and then, before our incredulous eyes, one by one against the rich green of the shadowed hollies, we picked out seven grey and white shapes and knew them to be deer.

We were down-wind, my clothes were of the kind that mix well with the moors and woods, Mr. Bundy has often been mistaken for a rabbit, so Bill, big and white, was our only anxiety. With difficulty, for the ecstatic, gamey odour of the deer was hot on the breeze, I kept him behind me, and never taking my eyes off the herd we slowly began the descent. Through the boggy ground in the dip we went, regardless of the mingled mud and water filling my shoes, spotting Bill's coat, and plastering the hair to Mr. Bundy's minute shanks so that they resembled the drumsticks of a chicken ; one prayer on our lips, one hope in our hearts—that the grey ladies of the trees would tarry awhile longer.

Why they stayed I cannot imagine, but stay they did although the big hind doing sentry spotted us almost at once. She dropped her hocks ready to make off, and raised her head so high that her long white neck and big white ears a-cock looked like an albino boa constrictor in a monstrous cravat, but she held her ground. Her six sisters were quite innocent of our approach, strolling from sun-pool to sun-pool, flicking white tails, scratching a lowered head with a delicately-pointed hindfoot, or nibbling at the young holly leaves as if there were no dog nor human being nearer than Salisbury. We were three parts of the way up the slope, and so near to them that, bad and feeble shot as I am, I could have hit the sentry with a pebble, before she gave the alarm, and the herd

55

melted away like magic. Unable to control Bill any longer I let him go, and with Mr. Bundy I examined the ground for slot; Mr. Bundy plainly thrilled to his very marrow by his first encounter with attar of venison.

We waited a while for Bill, but as he did not come back we left the little covert and climbed on to the moor behind it. Here we found trees on either hand: Studley's oaks and pines to the left, the pines of Franchise Wood away on the right, and seedling pines sprouting all over the plain. Two small ponds, probably dry in summer, lay side by side on the left of the track, and as we neared them I rejoiced to see Bill come bounding over the heather towards us. His jaws gaped so widely that it looked as if his head were in two halves, and yards of dripping tongue lolled between them. His beatific smile sobered when he saw me but I had not the heart to be angry with him, and so, quickly recovering his spirits, he plunged into the pools, drinking and splashing, while Mr. Bundy scolded from the bank. He cannot bear Bill to risk death by drowning.

When Bill had recovered his breath and had shaken himself over us we went on, still keeping to the left until the track led us to Studley's north gate. Here it forked and we took the right fork. On its way it goes under an arch of hollies, thorns, and oaks, almost immediately afterwards passes through a gateway of high gorse bushes, and then links up with the hard gravel track running to Hampton Ridge. At this point Hope Cottage, the white, thatched little building at the meeting of the Downton and Fordingbridge roads, showed on the right.

A FOREST POOL

For a while as we walked we had the Dorset hills ahead of us, looking very splendid across the pine-sown heath, but on taking the Islands Thorns track on our left we quickly lost sight of the neighbouring county as the gorse grows high and close on every side, and where there is a gap a young larch is sure to step in. Here, obviously, was excellent covert for any game, and Bill was soon racing off with ears up and straight tail, aware in every fibre of what it held. We lost sight of him at once, but hearing him thrashing round in the bushes we kept our eyes open.

Quite suddenly there was a sharp 'thut, thut!'; a gorse bush close on our left swayed, crackled, and out of its heart burst a deer, only to sail over the track and disappear into the open arms of the bush's opposite number, and be lost as completely as though she had been saved from Bill as Daphne was from Apollo. Bill arrived gaping, grinning and bewildered a second after, was congratulated but put on the lead, as much for his own sake as that of the deer.

At Islands Thorns the path is met in state, a canopy of short oaks, big hollies and handsome thorns growing over it as if preparing it for the woodland mansion it is about to inherit.

The trees of Islands Thorns are tall and thin, but they grow so closely that the wood looks somehow full of mist and the sun slants through the trunks in narrow streaks. The ride, though, is wide and open to the sun, grassy and garnished with bunches of bracken and bramble good for a rabbit as a rule, though all were abroad that day. We followed along, turning neither to left nor right until we

57

reached a gravel track stuck with telegraph poles. This we went up left-handed and were carried by it over two more of Latchmore brook's headsprings, out into the main track from Amberwood and the Ridge.

On reaching Fritham we met a man pointing stakes, and assuming as nonchalant an air as possible remarked to him that the deer seemed to be moving about pretty freely that morning. To our secret elation he got quite excited, made us say how many and where exactly we had seen the herd, and then told us that people may live a lifetime in the Forest and not come across a single deer. I asked him why he thought the deer waited for us to come so close, and he said it was because we had kept moving. If we had stood still when the sentinel deer saw us she would have raced the herd away at once. He also said the trees of Islands Thorns were only planted in 1850, which would account for their poor growth, and then I remembered that there used to be a pottery there in Roman-British days which turned out a superior ware to that made in the Sloden potteries. He said that was so, and Mr. Sumner could tell me all about it, and then asked me what kind of dog was Bill. On learning he nodded with a shy smile towards Mr. Bundy and said, ' Well, well ! and whatever might that little thing be ? ' If Mr. Bundy's feelings were bruised he hid them manfully.

II

Snow took us by surprise on the night following that mild and smiling day. Such days, when they come un-expectedly in the winter months, are known in the Forest as ' weather breeders,' for they are almost invariably followed by something of even sterner stuff than that which had preceded them.

As the snow-dusted heights of the Forest looked so splendid from our window we decided to pay Fritham another visit and surprise the pool in a very different mood from that in which we had seen it so far. Thinking, too, that the Godshill uplands would never appear finer than when lying white under a grey sky, we packed ourselves into Miss Riley and set out for Fritham.

But long before we got there the sun was master of the heavens again, and a racing wind had not only swept away the clouds but had also driven the lightly fallen snow off nearly all the high places, allowing it to lie only on the sheltered slopes and in the hollows.

The pool being quite protected on all sides had not lost its snow and looked more lovely than we had ever seen it. The dazzling whiteness of its banks made the poor swan look anything but at his best, however, so we hurried away feeling quite embarrassed on his account.

Both dogs love the snow, though Bill cuts no better figure against it than the swan did, so they became jubilant directly I had removed their jackets. They are self-conscious to a painful extent when wearing these garments, which are home-made. Wakey and the odd man constructed Bill's out of an old horse-blanket, but Wakey alone was responsible for Mr. Bundy's natty knitted jumper with a polo collar.

We struck across the hillside till we got into Fritham's centre track and entered Islands Thorns. Turning right

59

we went up the telegraph-poled ride, following it over the two streams, up, down, and finally up and out on to the manly country of the Ridge.

We wanted to get to Godshill through Stone Quarry Bottom, visiting Pitt's Wood on the way, and this we could have done just as well by continuing with the telegraph poles. But we love the Ridge and did not want to leave it quite so soon, so we bore left and got into the track which heads for its northern slope and drops into Pitt's Wood by the southern hatch-gate.

To our joy we found snow still covering the shoulders that the hills had turned from the wind, lying in the ruts of the track, and here and there caught in the tiny heather branches. In spite of the sun the wind had a sharp edge, and glad to have it at our backs we hurried on, thankful when we dropped down the hillside that it remained on top.

A belt of conifers growing closely on the wood's boundary shields the valley oaks, and just inside the gate a host of silky young Douglas firs are massed as a further protection. The few oaks, which as thoughtless acorns planted themselves on the brow of the Ridge, are a tragic warning to any tree foolhardy enough to think of braving the merciless weather which sometimes rides that upland in winter. They stand gaunt skeletons along the track, their branches either petrified in a last gesture of despair or else snapped off short as though they had been no thicker than matchsticks.

Though our map shows the track tunnelling under trees it really skirts them, giving us a fine view of the oaks

60

towering up impressively above the bracken and holly bushes. The trees are over one hundred and fifty years old, having been planted in 1775.

On the other side of the track axe and saw have been at work apparently, and a tangle of rank grass, bracken and bramble have sprung up. As we crossed the stream in the hollow a fox advertised his presence by tainting the air with his unmistakable scent, but we saw no sign of him.

From the stream the track mounts up to Ashley Lodge and its outbuildings. They are built on a fence-encircled green, crossed by the track which passes between the cottage and the stable. There is no way round. Judge of our dismay then when we found a clearly printed notice on the gate saying 'No Dogs Allowed.' Fixing the lead to Bill's collar and tucking Mr. Bundy under my arm, an indignity he hates, I summoned up my courage and went through the gate in some trepidation. The young keeper was lounging in the stable door watching his baby play with a kitten. Emboldened by his peaceful air I asked him about the dog notice, and he said it only applied to the months of May and June when he was rearing young pheasants. He also told me that two days ago he had seen three red deer at the brook above the cottage. After admiring a litter of baby pigs, pink as dog roses, which were busily drawing nourishment from their dreadful parent in a nearby sty, we said goodbye and departed through another gate also bearing the dog notice.

It had been a shock to find that the pheasant plague, virulent as foot and mouth disease we think, had spread to the Forest, and for some way we brooded a trifle glumly over the discovery. Pheasant shooting has closed so many woods and fields to perfectly harmless folk, and by so doing has bred a great deal of the bitterness growing up between rich and poor. An example of its callousing influence on the human heart is the story we read in the church of Barford-St.-Martin lying below the downs covered by Grovely Wood.

Early in the nineteenth century one of the Pembrokes decided to turn the wood into a pheasant preserve. To do this successfully meant that he must stop the villagers from coming to it to gather dead wood for firing, a right to which they claimed to be entitled from time immemorial. Evidently 'preferring pheasants to peasants,' as a cotton manufacturer once said of himself to my father, he forbade the villagers to ' go sticking ' on pain of imprisonment. Although it meant a cold winter for them, as the average wage was seven and sixpence and did not permit of much coal buying, the villagers were too frightened to stand up for their right and gave way without a word : all except four women whose names are worthy to rank with those of Garibaldi and William Tell. Fanny Pomeroy, Anne Hibberd, and Sarah Abrahams, led by Grace Reed, decided to go up against the pride and power of the Pembrokes, establish their right to the dead wood of Grovely or ' die in the attempt.' Caught, they were tried and imprisoned, but not for long. A deed turned up proving them to have fought a just war and they were liberated. Though Grace Reed lies in the village churchyard we could not find her headstone. Perhaps she has not got one, nor her three fellow-warriors either, wherever they may sleep. But they have their memorial in the little processions going and coming daily to and from Grovely Woods, where, thanks to their pluck, the poor may gather wood to their hearts', or rather their hearths', content, to this day. If the peacock stands for pride, we thought, then the badge of selfishness is the pheasant.

At the top of the hill we regained our good spirits, gloomy thoughts melting away at the glorious sight of miles of sunlit, snow-streaked hills on every hand. A sudden bend in the track revealed below us the billowy valley holding Pitt's Wood, with thorns and holly squads on every knoll beyond the wood, and the Ridge rising grandly above. We grew ecstatic; there seemed no end to the surrounding hills, to be more sky than usual; the air made us think of the sea-downs of Dorset.

Across the plain the track drops down by hollies and yews into Stone Quarry Bottom, crosses Ditchend brook and flicks like a whiplash up the slope along whose top the cars fly to Fordingbridge or Southampton.

Below the bridge the brook widens into a pool on the frozen surface of which Bill at once ventured. He loves to watch his reflection running along below him, but had to go unsatisfied on this occasion, as the thin ice bent and cracked so alarmingly that we thought Mr. Bundy's worst fears would be realised.

The summit of the opposite slope attained, the tarmac had to be followed in spite of the cars; but it did not last long, and the way was beguiled for us by a man with a faggot-laden cart drawn by one of the heavier type of

63

Forest-bred cobs. The man had a frizzed Alexandra fringe and talked to us about the cob, whose flat knees, clean legs and hard condition belied its twenty-two years. It was, he said, a temperamental animal, with strong likes and dislikes. He had bred and broken it himself and was the only one to handle it till he went to the War. During his absence the hired man employed by his parents to do his work found on attempting to work the horse that he ' couldn't do nothin' wi' en, did'n know what to make of 'en, got prarper upsides wi'en, for 'en couldn't never do wi' strangers, look.' This the old rogue bore out when I tried to rub his grey muzzle, tossing his head away contemptuously and burying his face in his master's coat. Our talk turned to dogs, and the young man said he preferred little dogs to big ones as they were generally more game, ' like little fellers,' he added, being a small man himself. He said he knew of a dog no bigger than Mr. Bundy which would go to ground after badger or fox and never came out alone !

We parted company at the 'Fighting Cocks' inn which stands on the outskirts of Godshill village, a community of arts and crafts, ' ye olde ' this and that, sandals, and no collars. In Sandyballs, a lovely hanging greenwood rising sheer above an arm of the Avon and adjoining the village, there is a close season when visitors are not allowed. At least I am told so, and this on account of a nudist colony which inhabits there during the summer. If this is so I hope for their sakes that the flies are less virulent in Sandyballs than elsewhere in the Forest. I doubt the truth of the story though, because not long ago I spent a

A GYPSY CAMP

delicious summer morning in the wood, and was guided along its enchanting rides by a youth unlike any I had met before.

To this day I cannot make up my mind whether he was what Stephen Langland would call one of ' God's boys ' or merely a product of the quaint village. I came across him combing a white rabbit at his cottage door and asked if he could tell me the way to Cerdic's Camp, an earthwork which I have since learnt is just outside Godshill Enclosure. He leapt to his feet, deposited the rabbit in a spotless cage, and volunteered to guide me. We never found the camp, because he kept stopping to gather wildflowers which he thrust into my hands laughing delightedly, or danced down a ride to show me how lovely the Avon looked through the tree-trunks, or darted through bushes to lead me to some nest he knew of. By the time we said goodbye I had not only an armful of flowers to stow into the car, but a young lilac tree and a young broom bush so cleverly uprooted that they flourish in our garden still.

At the back of the ' Fighting Cocks ' a lane runs down a steep hill, crosses Millersford brook at the bottom and then mounts swiftly between gorsey banks to Godshill Enclosure. A wide strip of turf runs along outside the enclosure, and this we followed because of the view on our right until we came to the second gate and then we entered the wood. A path, sprouting with whortleberry and decorated with trailing ivy, meanders between tall oaks, pines, and sweet chestnuts until it falls in with a ride. This we turned down right-handed, following it to the lodge on the Woodgreen road. We left the wood with regret, for though there is no very impressive timber to look at, the hill only having been planted in 1810, it has big clearings revealing such visions of trees climbing up one slope, pouring down others, filling hollows, and capping the rises beyond that we were almost persuaded to spend the rest of the morning in the enclosure.

At the gate we turned right; a left turn would have taken us to Woodgreen, a village with a charming setting but no architectural graces. The lane we entered has generous grass borders growing gorse and holly and runs between Godshill and Densham woods. As we neared its end a wondrous equipage rounded the corner, driven by a delightful lady. It consisted of a seat with back and dashboard, mounted on two motor-car wheels, whose balloon tyres made the smartly trotting donkey between the shafts appear more slender than he was. A gentlemanly greyhound brought up the rear.

We found ourselves out on the green track skirting Godshill Enclosure, turned left, and so towards Millersford Bottom. Before descending into that churlish valley of scrubby trees, coarse grass, bramble and bog, we stopped on the brow of the hill to look at the fine bluff of Turf Hill and its pines, the ridge carrying the Fordingbridge road, Hampton Ridge and the intervening crest, and the mazy dance of hills still farther ahead.

At the bottom of the track a grubby but kind old man sucking a clay pipe told us how to manage the passage of Millersford brook, whose wet fingers spread out over the green fording place and make it into a bog, not dangerous but messy. The old man's pipe reminded me of a story

66

told me by a friend whose husband had proffered his
tobacco pouch to a tramp at the door. The offer was
politely refused, the tramp saying he had plenty of
' Universal Roadside Shag.' He showed the inviting mixture, and explained that it was made of the cigarette ends
he had picked up, robbed of their paper bands, and neatly
shredded and packed into his tin.

Across the stream we went up a path on the left, passed
a wood displaying trespasser boards, swung up the snow-
filled curve of Turf Hill's flank, went under the pines
throwing long blue shadows over the snow, and in no
time were on top of the plain. Straight ahead and easily
recognisable by its belt of pines lay Telegraph Hill.

Early in the nineteenth century there was a chain of
semaphore stations running from Plymouth to London.
Each station was on a high hill, and Bramshaw Telegraph,
to give it its correct name, was one of them. It is 419 feet
high and commands miles of glorious country ; from it
one looks across Hampshire's last woods and valleys to
the Wiltshire hills on the north, to Dorset's abundant
downs on the south-west, and to the Isle of Wight over
the whole breadth of the Forest on the south.

The track by which we gained Bramshaw Telegraph,
via the heathery plain on top of Turf Hill, had put us
down on the road to Wiltshire Downton just short of its
meeting with the Fordingbridge road and Hope Cottage.
The choice of routes to Fritham from Telegraph Hill is
great. You can go to the village through the woods or
over the moors or down the Southampton highway, which
you must leave when you come to either of the gravel

roads on the right. Both roads cross Longcross Plain, the lower one going down to Irons Well, the upper one to Fritham House on Jane's Moor.

We crossed the Fordingbridge road just below the Downton fork, and entering a track that goes through Black Gutter Bottom and over the gutter's headsprings quickly got into the track leading to Amberwood.

CHAPTER V

TWO MORE WALKS
FROM FRITHAM

THE road turning away from the powder factory and passing Irons Well on the right is as charming as we knew it would be. The only drawback is that it is much too short. The hanging wood of beech and oak it disappears into so soon is as soon forsaken for the airy uplands of Longcross Plain, up which it starts to climb at once. We had barely time to think how lovely the massed woods, Eyeworth, Islands Thorns, and Studley looked from over the way, or to appreciate the pleasant shelter provided for the deer by the clumps of mingled hollies and other trees dotting the slopes beyond them, before a brave upward curve of the road landed us high on a bit of level going, and we saw with a shock a scarlet petrol lorry flying down what we had taken to be a heathery, lonely hillside, recognised the pines behind it as those of Franchise Wood, and knew ourselves to be already confronted with the Southampton road.

We negotiated the highway, exchanging it for the less frequented road crossing Black Bush plain, which lies at the top of Piper's Weight, a hill standing 422 feet high and commanding a magnificent stretch of country. All round are woods and lesser heights, and over them in the far distance the smooth curves of the Island show; nearer at hand rise the Wiltshire hills with their creamy fields and purple-brown coverts.

The road goes winding steeply down, runs for a bit along the fringe of Bramshaw Wood, whose trees supplied Salisbury Cathedral with timber, and then comes up on to the green of No Man's Land. From here the foreign

70

hills look very close, and quell the ugly little houses trying
to get in their way. In the shop, at whose counter I
bought some of the best acid drops ever sucked, we were
told that the four small squares on the green were quoit
bases, that the bald patch in the middle was the cricket
pitch, and that the road crossing the green and entering
the trees leads into the thoroughfare which travels along
the boundary of the Forest and joins the Southampton
road at Brook. I believe, but cannot be certain, that the
village came by the odd name of No Man's Land in the
following manner. When the Forest was being divided
into walks, each with a keeper to watch over it, this part was
forgotten and no one was made responsible for it. Thus
it became first No Man's Walk and later No Man's Land.

A track goes right-handed through Bramshaw Wood
from the green, but by following it one turns one's back
on the hills of Wiltshire ; we kept to the road because it
shows them through the tree trunks nearly all the way.
The oaks and beeches on either hand are big and well
grown, the beeches bright with patches of moss and held
to the ground by knuckle-like mossed roots, the oaks
scorning any decoration other than the fine linework of
their bark. Though we dawdled it was not long before
we were walking along the boundary road between the
free woods of the Forest and the fence-hampered country
which begins almost as soon as the Forest ends.

Bramshaw's church is on an isolated tree-covered knoll,
skirted by the road ; its tower houses a plain little bell,
cast in the days when Norman kings were still hunting
in the Forest.

About a quarter of a mile farther along we came to the fringe of the village and turned up a tree-shaded lane on the right. It joined a road which climbed uphill through beautiful beeches and oaks, over patches of treeless ground until it reached the Southampton highway. We crossed the highway about half a mile above where we had crossed it on leaving the Irons Well road, and went right along the top of Longcross plain, with the twin woods of Salisbury Trench and Linwood Copse on our left.

Fritham House we left on our right, and kept steadily on up the road across Jane's Moor. Just short of Stony Cross we turned right-handed into the track heading for Ocknell Enclosure across Stoney Cross Plain.

Here on the plain it was ' off leads and away ' for the dogs, who for several miles now had patiently ambled along attached to these apron strings. Before following in their flying footsteps I had to stop for a bit and drink my fill of the free and far-flung loveliness all round. Woods, valleys, and hills rolled away as far as eye could follow, sunlit and mottled with the speedy shadows of the spring clouds ; without moving a foot or losing sight of the lark exulting overhead I visited the smooth downs of the Isle of Wight, Wiltshire, and the heights which hold Romsey Abbey in the hollow of their hand.

Mr. Bundy having returned in some anxiety to see what had happened to me, I went along with him towards where Ocknell Enclosure's outer-defences come up to the rim of the trough it fills to overflowing with its oaks and beeches. The track, a beauty, wide and sound as a bell nearly all the way, heads straight for the noblest group of pines we know in the north of the Forest. They soar up on flawless trunks, dwarfing the other trees, themselves of no mean stature, and sway their dark plumes proudly above the pacific green polls of their neighbours. Mr. Sumner thinks that they are probably the first of their kind to be planted in the Forest. Pines apparently had died out here, though in the days of the mastodon they flourished in this part. Then in the eighteenth century some one thought of experimenting, and when Ocknell's oaks and beeches were planted in 1775 these pines were set on the bluff above them.

Now the track, while it leaves nothing to be desired as regards surface, exasperates by never staying long under the trees. As Mr. Bundy says, ' When we decide to walk through a wood we mean a wood, not a chain of covert and forest, forest and covert.' It enters the trees by the pines, curves past them, drops downwards and struggles upwards under bosky arches and over open heathy bits, crosses by means of good bridges the twin headsprings of Highland Water and at the last of these bridges it starts on its last climb. This time it stays with the trees until Ocknell Plain is reached, and once among them we agreed they were worth waiting for. They are none of them weaklings, and whether they grow tall and straight, or start to thrust out big branches before they are five feet from the ground, they are all sound and of considerable girth ; grand old things, with here and there a few really notable specimens, such as the three holly trees, big as young beeches, half-way up on the right, and the massive oak just above them. His branches grow out of his head like the tentacles of a nightmare squid, and are wrapped in moss and generously ferned.

Ocknell Plain is wild and lonely, but neither bleak nor forbidding; it is high, peaceful, overlooks the quiet woods surrounding it, and is never forsaken for long by holm bushes. But its supreme grace is its pond, which, renouncing the things of this world, lies unshadowed by bush or tree, reflecting heaven only.

Two good tracks cross outside the wood, but neither leads directly to the pond. It is easily and quickly reached, however, if you go straight across the heather, steering a course between an important knot of hollies ahead and a scattering of insipid young pines on the right. It was a great moment for us when we came upon it for the first time where it lay amongst the dusky heather in its magic circle of bright, short grass, peacefully contemplating the sky. On its breast it wears a tussock of coarse sedge as a kind of hair shirt we think, for had it hankered after gay trappings the gilded gorse and green and silver holly would never have been banished from its marge.

Bill, being no respecter of persons, turned the chaste pool into a bathing pool, frolicking through it in an ecstasy of fooling and scattering its water to the winds in glittering showers. We watched him, I laughing, Mr. Bundy disapprovingly, until the wretched fellow turned his attention to us, left the pool, circled us rapidly, stopped dead and then shook himself with devastating wetness all over us.

On this we left the pond, Mr. Bundy muttering in his beard, I definitely soured and Bill quite unashamed.

The plain is crossed by a gravel road running from Linwood to Stony Cross Plain, but as it is very seldom used its presence does not spoil the peace of Ocknell and Broomy Plains which it divides.

Just across the road, near the knot of hollies that guided us to the pond, is a track going through the heather to Holly Hatch Enclosure, in whose secret groves the lily of the valley blows. The wood shares with Broomy the love of the deer, and it was in the hopes of seeing some that we set out for it. But our luck was out, as we knew at once when we saw that the enclosure gate was propped open and then noted the newly churned wheel tracks in the rides. To our further chagrin we heard the spitting and spluttering of a motor-tractor somewhere below and realised that amends in the shape of muscular teams of timber-hauling horses were not to be made to us.

As is so often the case in the Forest the enclosure is framed by pine trees, but for the most part oaks, more tall than broad and of no great robustness, cover its slopes and knolls. There are good tracks in plenty, some grass, some gravel, and all with a sprinkling of brown leaves and occasionally of the spiny bonnets of chestnuts.

We continued down the gravel track by which we entered the wood, as we wanted to come out by the lodge opposite Old Sloden's hill. Bill became insufferably jaunty as we neared the lodge, his head full of the amiable spaniel maiden he had met there once before. But at the lodge Mr. Bundy and I got our own back, for, instead of the dusky maid, Bill was confronted by a crusty old dog

75

beagle who had nothing but surly answers to his crest-fallen enquiries.

Instead of following the track over Dockenswater (here called Broomywater) up the hill, through Sloden to Fritham, we turned sharp right and walked along the grass ride between the stream and Holly Hatch till we got to Anses through the tangle of thorns, heather, and bracken flourishing on its outskirts.

Anses is old and gobliny, and beautiful, too. Crab apples, hollies, oaks, and beeches grow together in rough confusion but perfect good fellowship on the slope between South Bentley and Holly Hatch. The oaks are all fine old trees, their bark gracefully diapered, their shape true to the best oak tradition; of the beeches this cannot always be said. Some heel over at perilous angles, others split into branches almost as soon as they stop being roots, and others, fallen, prop themselves on some great limb and continue to bear leaf and mast as if nothing had happened. They suffer, too, from a curious infirmity of purpose with regard to their branches, a malady most incident to beeches and called ingrowth. Thus a tree may grow to normal length of stem and start to branch like its neighbour, but after the limbs are three to four feet long they will reunite, become completely fused, and then after another foot or so will break away and behave perfectly naturally for the rest of their lives. It appears impossible, too, for one branch to touch another without becoming locked in an inseparable, if brief, embrace.

After a diverting few minutes of freak-branch hunting we went up a spongy ride and came out on to the plain opposite the Ocknell pond knot of hollies. Bearing left we went through the heather and joined the track that gets to Fritham through North and South Bentley enclo- sures. These oak woods have great beauty and the proud reputation of providing the best grown timber in this part of the Forest.

At the bottom of the track we found ourselves in a lovely green hollow lying in a half-circle of hillside woods, and watered by the Dockens stream, here in its infancy. Facing us was the road which, with a cottage or two at its edge, climbs up the hill to Fritham and skirts the green on its way to the ' Royal Oak.'

II

This road led us one day to take a most successful walk. Even the absence of Mr. Bundy, who was laid up with bronchitis, could not mar its beauty. The green hollow looked even better when approached from Fritham, and as we went slowly up through the Bentleys we found they also looked more beautiful from this side, and noticed, too, that there are quite a lot of beeches among the oaks and that many of them have ferns as well as moss on them. Just before the plain is reached the trees thin out and leave the hollies and a few less particular oaks and beeches to make what they can of a boggy waste, glittering with runnels in some parts but mostly thickly covered with heather. Though the trees grow low, as if afraid to show their branches above the shelter of the slope, the heather grows so high that Bill found it necessary to leap up and down in it like a Jack-in-the-box to see where he was

77

going. Even then it contrived a booby-trap for him, screening a deep pool so cleverly that he dropped straight into it without the slightest suspicion of its being there.

Out on the plain we turned right and kept to tracks whose meanderings never went far from the woods which cover the slopes all the way to Linwood. The whole way along there are splendid views to the right; on the left the plain's hollies and the pines of Slufters and Milkham Enclosures shut out the country beyond.

Soon after leaving the Bentleys, and as soon as the plain is reached, Fritham Plain's pale holly-studded flank shows up between South Bentley and Anses. Then Holly Hatch, as we near it, blots out Fritham Plain, but it re-appears, carrying the first oaks and yews of Old Sloden, when the track swings out again to the left. At every break in the trees, at every outward bearing of the path, the views grow in grandeur. The most compelling of them all we came upon suddenly from behind a bunch of young pines growing on the brow of a slope below which Holly Hatch and Broomy meet and dip. Above them the two hills bearing Old Sloden and Hasley sail majestically into sight in a colourful sea of ridges whose farthest crest is merged with the skyline somewhere in Wiltshire.

At the end of about two miles of moorland wandering the path ends at a gravel track going downhill to Broomy Lodge. I am not sure whether Broomy Lodge is the private house hidden by the trees of Broomy or the cottage standing on the wood's edge. The cottage has a few outbuildings beside it, and nothing in front of it but a green with a few yews and hollies ; it is half-way up the hillside, and below it in the valley are a couple of fields, an orchard, and a stream. We descended into the valley, crossed the brook, climbed up past the cottage and the white iron gate of the hidden house, and were soon on top of the hill. From here we recognised with delight, across a thorn-filled valley and High Corner wood, our old acquaintances Whitefield Plantation and Ibsley Common. Then we went down again, catching more glimpses of Hasley and his valley of hills, jumped an unbridged water-course running over a grassy bottom, and entered a green path that goes close against Broomy's railings.

Bill had had no luck with his hunting, and so when we came across a plump yearling colt all by itself among the gorse bushes he tried to play with it. But the colt, after gazing at him owlishly for a little bit, uttered a whimpering neigh and toddled off like a spoilt child. Fortunately I had made Bill come to heel, for in answer to the colt's cry his mama came briskly on the scene, looking anything but pleasant, and accompanied by a very wobbly foal not many days old. However, her looks belied her, and instead of bearing down on Bill and striking out at him with death-dealing fore-feet she contented herself with comforting her frightened son.

It is not unusual to come across these little family parties of mother and two youngsters in the Forest. Nowadays the pasture is not nearly as plentiful as it used to be, and there are two reasons for this state of affairs.

Firstly, the destruction of the deer; secondly, the spread of seedling pines. Deer eat down undergrowth that no pony will touch, thus giving the grass a chance to grow where, but for them, a mass of thorn trees and bushes would cover the ground. There being insufficient deer to deal with them the bushes are thriving almost as well as the seedling pines. Where the little pines grow nothing will feed, and as they are allowed to spread unhindered, and spread like wildfire, they are rapidly ruining some of the best feeding-grounds the ponies have. So it is that many mares with newly-dropped foals are still suckling yearlings which, growing and hungry, supplement their menu with their mothers' milk, being unable to pick up enough grass and furze-tops to satisfy their appetites. No wonder the mares in question are ' all bones and belly.'

Though the brood mares are often a sorry sight it is seldom one sees a working pony in anything but good, hard condition. Their owners, even if they have not bred them, have often bought them as suckers for a few shillings, reared them, and broken them in themselves. Many of these ponies have never smelt an oat in their lives, but of what they do get they are not stinted. Sometimes their diet is a mixture one would have thought more suitable for fowls or pigs. One pony I know, a game little roan, is fed on potatoes, meal and turnips, cooked and mashed. I should have thought such a menu disastrous, but he looks fine on it. The owner of a really poor pony is conscious that his neighbours sneer at him, for they do their sneering openly and loudly. I myself heard a

New Forest Ponies

contemptuous voice cry outside my window not long ago, ' Harse? that's not a harse; that's an iron 'ardle!' Looking out I saw the owner of the ' iron hurdle ' drive by ; his face was the colour of a new villa.

To make up for his disappointment over the foal Bill found a squirrel in the bracken, and had a brisk sprint after it to a pine tree just inside Broomy's rails. Half-way up the trunk the entrancing little thing paused to look coolly down at his pursuer, hopelessly leaping up and down below. He stayed long enough for me to notice how perfectly his coat matched the variegated bark of the pine, and then slipped out of sight round the trunk. I knew if we waited long enough he would come out again to see what we were doing, for squirrels are as curious as monkeys, and before long he ran along a branch from which he could see us safely and easily. Silhouetted against the pale sky, so that his pointed ears, blunt little face, his tiny, lithe body and cloudy tail stood out clearly, he really was an enchanting imp. I could have watched him at his fussy antics for as long as he would have waited, but the knocking of hub against axle, announcing that a timber cart, hidden and otherwise soundless, was bumping down upon us along a green ride, sent me away for his sake. In the Forest they eat squirrels, hunting the poor little beasts from tree to tree, and when the chance offers knocking them off their perches with lead-weighted sticks called squoyles, which they throw with wonderful success.

Like most creatures who suffer from curiosity squirrels become friendly very quickly. A friend of mine who lives near some pinewoods in Norfolk found that while con-

F   81

suming his early morning tea he was being watched by a family of squirrels who had their drey in the pines close to the house. After a long time and great patience he got them to come into his room, and at last they became so friendly that they fed from his hand and played about his floor like kittens. The only drawback to this friendship was that he never dared to get out of bed until they had gone because they so often mistook his toes for nuts !

I, too, had a squirrel friend, but he was a foreigner and our friendship was as brief as it was sweet. I saw him sitting hunched up all alone in an old parrot cage outside a live-stock dealer's in Camden Town. In similar cages near him portly fellows of his kind were crammed in sixes and sevens, bickering and fooling like schoolboys. He looked so lonely and so sad I bought him, cage and all, for seven shillings and sixpence and carried him back to my rooms. I was told he came from the Hartz mountains, so I thought his gloom was homesickness, and this belief was strengthened when, after a bad beginning, marked by bitten fingers and terrified efforts to escape, he suddenly became contented and even happy. He got really fond of me and ran about the room freely, only going to his cage at nights or when I was out. My meals he shared, sitting by my plate and carefully examined each mouthful I wished to eat, laying a gentle, detaining paw on my hand while he waved his whiskers over the morsel it held. If it was something he liked he helped himself neatly, if not he sat back on his haunches and merely stroked his whiskers. Unhappily he soon began to sicken, and before three weeks had passed I found him one morning lying dead in the hay nest he had made in his cage.

From Broomy we went across Ogden's Purlieu, keeping on till we reached the Ridge, and so to Fritham through Amberwood.

CHAPTER VI

THE RUFUS STONE

W E now knew something of all the roads that meet at the 'Royal Oak,' except the more conventional one that comes down from the high plain behind the village. For although we had arrived by it every time we came to Fritham we had done so by car, and you cannot say you really know a road until you have walked it. By car you only get to know it in the same way as you get to know the stations on the line you travel along regularly.

This road when walked, for instance, at once becomes longer and more winding, its hills more steep, its descents more precipitate. From the walker it has no secrets, but gladly shows him, over gateway and through gap, charming and intimate views of field, farm, and cottage, withheld from the motorist. The pond in the crook of its elbow below Fritham House looks much bigger from the brink and is always offering hospitality to something nice in the way of bird or beast, even going so far as to treat pig matrons to mud masks free of charge.

The road divides at the pond : one branch passing round it goes straight on to Jane's Moor; the other, continuing its original course, joins the moor road by a cottage where violets and snowdrops grow all together in the garden, and a handsome, silky, parti-coloured dog basks before a kennel. The mistress of the cottage is a dear, not only anxious but able to direct one's steps aright through the woods and over the moors.

On Jane's Moor is a pond and two ancient grave mounds, one of which is covered with bushes and has a pine tree growing out of the top. To reach it one goes

86

round by the pond, and this we did because, although the cottage road would have taken us more quickly to Linwood Copse through which we intended walking, we wanted to have a look at the mound first.

When we got to it we found a nice old man with a grey moustache neatly clipped and a mahogany-coloured face mending the road near it. Close by in the lee of a gorse bush his tricycle stood, sheltered from sudden showers by a huge gig umbrella whose knobbly handle was wedged in the wheel-spokes to keep it true to its trust.

I asked him the name of the mound, whereupon he rested his folded arms on his spade, and fixing me with his benign eyes began slowly and patiently as follows:

'That there is Jane's Moor Butt, and all this round here,' with a sweep of the arm, 'is Jane's Moor. Now in the old days we was always fighting of the French, look. They French kep' on trying for to land, and mostly we kep' pushen' of 'en off. But sometimes, look, they did just manage to get on shore and then there was fighten' arl over this Forest. Now they do say as how Jane's Moor Butt and that other butt you can see just further along, be Frenchmen's graves, but, of course, I can't say for certain, 'twas all so long ago and I wasn't about them days.' Thus he denied some ancient British warriors their graves, and went on to tell how wonderful the air was up on the plain, speaking with quite patriotic fervour. 'Well! the old people yere,' he said with pride, 'you'd never 'ardly credit. Why people as comes visiting up yere and sees them walken' about—80, 84, 92, and 96 or 7, or so—well it makes them say as how they wished

87

they might be able to come and live yere, too. And then the honey ! They do say as how our honey has more virtue for healing and that than any other soever.'

We found it hard to leave him, but we had not long for our walk, and so, thanking him and bidding him good morning, we crossed the moor road just opposite Fritham House and were soon under the beeches, oaks, and hollies that make the threshold of Linwood Copse so spacious and so pleasant. The trees are so tall that the birds' voices gain in their branches the echoing clarity a boy's treble takes to itself in an empty cathedral choir.

Beeches must have a sense of humour. They spread their silver branches so beautifully against their brilliant transparent leafage that you cannot choose but gaze upwards as you walk. Then, through the brown leaves of many autumns lying deep on the ground below them, they thrust their roots in curves exactly calculated to fit the human toe. The result, as I know to my cost, is frequently quite shattering.

Set in an angle of the ugly iron-band fence we found the gate we were looking for and the ride that would take us to Brook Common. The wood being on a hillside the ride runs down at once grassy, bracken and bramble-strewn, and patched with gravel where the trees stand back from it, softer and mossy as it gets lower and pushes its way through the heart of the wood. The beeches and oaks share the honours here, sometimes coming in groups but for the most part mingling indiscriminately. They have none of the dignity of the beeches outside the enclosure, growing to no great height, being scraggily branched when oaks and stumpily stemmed when beeches. Perhaps the beeches have been pollarded; they look to me as if they had suffered this indignity, but then I am no judge of these things.

The wood has an unkempt air, and its undergrowth is a wild tangle of rank grass and bramble, with a curiously deserted look about it as though no little beasts made their homes among it. But if the underscrub is without friends the trees have green lovers in plenty. Ivy sends delicate sprays darting up their trunks, moss wraps itself about root and branch, and ferns grow profusely on the sunward curve of those tree-trunks which, either from some infirmity due to age or some handicap in youth, have not been able to hold up their heads. One oak, growing tall and straight as a lance before its branches begin, wears a shoulder-knot of ferns in the fork of one of them.

The track ends abruptly on the curve of another, hard and gravelly, with a bridge to right and left, and ferns and heather at its edges. Under the bridges run two tiny streams, so small that they are called gutters. They join later, and then are called King's Garn Gutter after the wood they pass on their way to Blackthorne Copse, at Canterton. Here they link up with Coalmere Gutter, a stream deserving a better name.

Had we gone left we should have reached the Southampton road through Salisbury Trench, the wood joining Linwood Copse. As it was we turned right, it being in our minds to get to Canterton over Brook Common and through one of the loveliest wooded bottoms in the Forest.

89

In spring the track is rather soft going under the trees but makes up for it at the clearings.

The gate at the end has a happy opening. The stream runs out a little below it, across the narrow neck of common are the thickly massed pines that frame King's Garn Enclosure, and sweeping up to the right is the broad drive which cuts King's Garn off from Linwood Copse and ends on top of Jane's Moor. From the top of this drive, as can well be imagined, the plain being nearly four hundred feet up and overlooking a wooded valley to the wooded heights of Wiltshire, one is given really inspiring views.

We turned away from the hill and followed a path which goes patiently over the petty ups and downs of the common, allows the stream to cross it under a sprawling lot of bushes, and rising abruptly and refreshed by its cool bath reaches the golf course by the putting-green whose scarlet tassel showed over the top of the little hill.

Not possessing the necessary diligence I am not a golfer, so I cannot say how the course stands with regard to that linguistic game, but from the standpoint of charm it must be difficult to beat. It lies at the feet of grandly rising hills and gentle slopes, all of them wooded, and is laid over a ripple of closely grazed turf with gorse and thorns and heather to give it variety. On top of the highest hill and showing up sharply above the softness of the climbing woods the hotel at Stony Cross is a good landmark.

At the end of the links is the cricket pitch, fenced off and mown by the teeth of any pony willing to oblige. It is all so peaceful and so pleasant that it is something of a shock to learn that one of the greens is said to mark the spot where a murderer hung in chains until a tipsy sailor cut him down one night for a bet. In Horace Hutchinson's charming book on the Forest he says one old man, who daily passed the hanging skeleton of his quondam acquaintance, thought it fun to tap the back of the skull so that he could see the tits fly out at the eye holes ! The crime for which the murderer suffered was callous as well as brutal. He robbed a poor old bedridden woman, set her cottage on fire while she was alive, and when he judged the fire had taken sufficient hold to make rescue impossible went to the police and told them the cottage was alight. The old woman, though dying when help arrived, was just able to tell the police how her home came to catch fire and so brought her murderer to his end.

A lane runs past the links to Canterton and is reached by going round the cricket pitch and heading for the raised tee under an arch of trees. Gaining the lane we went along between neatly cut-and-laid fences, with Skers Farm and its fields on the left and privately owned Blackthorn Copse, spoilt by its unfriendly notice boards, on the right. I have been told that a mediæval water-mill worked by Coalmere Gutter stood in the copse at the time of the Domesday Survey, and that its site is still marked by the earthworks it stood upon.

We crossed the stream by an elevated, superior bridge, and soon found ourselves at Canterton.

It is not a village and one can hardly call it a hamlet, even though it has a manor house and an inn called the ' Sir Walter Tyrrel.' There is also a pretty old whitened brick-and-timber farm with a small orchard, a roadside pond, a big tin Dutch barn, and some unfortunate modern additions. Its rather pathetic fields lie in front of it, and in one, a bit higher up the road, is a fine pine tree. There are a good many handsome pines in Canterton, but this one is the handsomest.

In the latter part of the twelfth century a man called Purkis lived here, and up till fairly recently—that is to say within living memory—the cottage of his descendants stood here on the actual site of his old hut. He got his living by charcoal burning, and no doubt helped himself when one of the royal bucks came within reach and no one else was about.

It was this humdrum fellow who came across the arrow-stuck body of William Rufus, lying cold, lonely and terrible in the oak grove just beyond the village. He must have had an abnormal amount of courage to have lifted the dead king on to his cart and bring him to Winchester.

It was only a matter of minutes before we had passed the inn and were standing by the iron-encased stone marking the place where the tree stood whose timely interference with Sir Walter's arrow did the country such signal service. The stone was set up and the history of the king's accident cut upon it by John Lord Delaware in 1745 when the tree itself died. Its strait-waistcoat was put on it only after nineteenth-century trippers had done it considerable damage.

The grove is not a lonely forsaken place where one can easily imagine the noise of the approaching hunt, the sudden appearance and turning to bay of the exhausted

RUFUS STONE

buck, the arrival of the horn-blowing hunters on their great sweating horses. But it can be done if one comes here early in the year, when the numerous paths and the track from the Stony Cross highway are free from trippers and no postcard-selling gypsies hang about the stone. Then, leaning against the stone undisturbed, one can at length get back to the second day of August in the year 1100, hear the high falsetto screeches with which men still encourage hounds come from the hunters as they fling themselves from the saddle, see Sir Walter take hasty aim, hear the angry buzz of the bowstring, watch the arrow leap away, glance off an oak, and speed straight to the heart of the king. How bewildered both buck and hounds must have been when the horsemen, suddenly scattering, thundered away through the trees, all except one who lay still on the ground because nobody had cried out, ' The bow is bent and drawn ; stand from the shaft.'

It was Rufus who enacted the death penalty for deer stealing, not the Conqueror, who ' loved the tall stags as if he was their father,' and so it was only fair that he should die for chasing one himself. The Conqueror was not more harsh than other men of his age, and as far as greed over game was concerned he compares very favourably with the landowner of our day. For his own pleasure he reserved the deer, wild boar, and hare, but he did not grudge the poor people rabbits and all winged game. If he ordered that dogs kept in the Forest should be lamed when big enough to bay a deer, he was more merciful than the man who allows his keeper to put down strychnine in coverts devoted to game. I know of a particularly

93

plucky and admirable terrier lost last summer in this way, the poor little brute dying in fearful and prolonged pain in spite of all the veterinary surgeon could do to save him.

The Conqueror has long and unjustly been under a cloud on account of the New Forest, and all because a parcel of disgruntled monks with a turn for fiction had got their knife into him. But nowadays no one really believes the stories of wrecked villages, homeless families, and burning churches which the monks saw fit to write down. For one thing, it is pretty obvious that if the Forest had been a thickly populated agricultural area when the Conqueror first came upon it it would not have struck him as being ideal country for the deer whose habits he knew so well. And for another thing, none of the people who have prodded the Forest for traces of the ruined villages has ever come across the slightest sign of them. Apart from all this, any self-respecting grain would give up the ghost if sown on the gravelled heights whose favourite children are gorse and heather, or in the boggy bottoms where sun dews and cotton grass get on so well.

We left the Rufus Stone by a rutty path across the hillside, and as we went had the lovely changing views of the wooded, heathy basin we had just left, to look at on our right. On the left the shoulder of the hill shuts out the country that rolls down through woodland and over moors to the sea.

Ahead of us was Stony Cross, one of the finest lookouts in the Forest. Besides a good hotel and a little guest house, called 'Dick Turpin's Cottage,' there are several cottages there, and a perfectly open cross-roads where cars frequently and disastrously collide.

Just before the first cottages are reached a track runs off to the right. We went down it, and leaving it for a narrow green path running downhill through the heather soon reached Long Beech Enclosure.

Once under the lovely old trees we went up a path which after a short climb dropped steeply to pass through a little stream, and then went uphill all the way until it reached Jane's Moor. Long Beech joins King's Garn, but where one begins and the other ends I do not know, nor does it matter at all that we can see because every foot of the way is delightful, whether it is under great branches or over clearings parti-coloured with bracken and heather. Birds abound in these woods, filling them with music and darting colours.

When we reached the end of the wood we saw Jane's Moor Pond lying some little way ahead between us and Fritham House. It is partly hedged by gorse, but mostly is open to the sun ; with ponies and cattle it is very popular as a shade.

Shade in the Forest tongue means exactly the opposite to what it does in ordinary speech ; it means a high, unsheltered place. Ponies are said to come to shade when they leave their lowland grazing grounds where they have been feeding through the early, dewy hours, and migrate to the high places where the flies are not. As soon as the sun is fairly up and doing the flies make the grassy bottoms and the woods impossible for the poor beasts, whose only course is to leave their grazing, go to the nearest shade and wait till the sun goes down ; then the flies, faithful as any sunflower, retire too.

There is one fly which, while it leaves the Forest ponies unmoved, drives the staidest newcomers frantic. It is an ugly, flat, grey brute, so hard that it is really difficult to kill in the ordinary way, and its method of tantalising its victims is to race over their hides like a tiny motor-car. It does not bite, but it tickles unbearably.

We know a Welsh pony of perfect manners and un-blemished character who became so frantic when visited by this pestiferous insect that his mistress, whose horse-mastery is of exceptional merit, almost despaired of him and began to think of sending him away. As he is very fast, sure-footed, intelligent, and a keen and clever jumper she decided that before parting with him she would resort to desperate remedies. Cribben Boy was turned loose in the Forest in the height of the fly-season and left to fight the flies alone. The experiment was a complete success, and the pony ignores them now as completely as my own Gay Lad did. I once discovered eighteen of the creeping jennies nestling together in the folds of soft skin between Gay Lad's thighs when I was ' flying ' him after a hack in the fly months ; he had not given any sign that he knew they were there !

We realise that several of the walks we have written down are by no means ten miles in length, but they have at least the merit of-taking one through nearly all the woods and over all the noblest moors in the north part of the Forest. There are villages we have not mentioned, and roads, too, simply because it has been our wish to

96

put before the walker the wild, quiet country where deer, fox, and birds are unused to being disturbed and are therefore more likely to be come upon unawares.

The neglected roads and villages will come into their own in a later chapter devoted to such things.

CHAPTER VII

THE GREAT WOODS

THE New Forest is divided up conveniently for our purpose into three parts by the highways linking Bournemouth with Lyndhurst, and Ringwood with Cadnam, a village on the Fordingbridge-Southampton road. Each of the three parts is entirely different in character from the other. North of the Ringwood road, a Roman one they say, the country is given to moors and hills; its woods are widely spaced, its streams never too wide to be accomplished by a single stride unless swollen by heavy rains. Directly the road is crossed the land begins to fall away, not swiftly in a sudden glissade but in a sequence of ridges by no means unimpressive in stature, though none of them is as high as Bramshaw Telegraph or Piper's Weight. The streams grow much bigger than the northern brooks, and develop pools in which, if not outsize in figure, one may bathe without fear of flooding the banks.

But the great feature of the ' middle area ' is its wealth of woods. They almost fill its heart, running in a practically unbroken mass from Burley to Lyndhurst. Beyond Lyndhurst they break up considerably, and though they do come together again as the Forest border is neared they never recapture their generous proportions nor their remoteness from human habitation.

In the centre woods it is possible to walk all morning and never once leave the trees. Such fine trees too ! And so hospitable that the morning spent among them will almost certainly be illumined by the appearance of some wild and lovely thing, either in fur or feather or on painted, downy wings.

Lots of people say that Lyndhurst is the best base for exploring the sylvan centre of the Forest ; others plump for Brockenhurst. But we would take off from Burley every time if we had to choose, for it is smaller and not so suburbanised and trippery as the other two. If it has contracted the scarlet fever of villadom, the symptoms, with becoming modesty, hide themselves behind the kind and tactful trees, leaving the village at least the appearance of simplicity.

Burley has grown up on the strip of road connecting the Ringwood and Bournemouth highways, and lies in a hollow between Picket Post and Markway Hill. Before it are the heathered wastes of Cranes Moor, Thorny Hill, and Holmesly, but behind it the great woods begin almost at once. On the rise above the ' Queen's Head ' is a mass of oaks and beeches, where hounds meet with their usual sure instinct for becoming backgrounds, and beyond is the golf course. Here a varied and interesting game is played, featuring mobile bunkers in the shape of cows and pigs, and putting-greens enlivened by amorous ponies.

Before retiring into the woods we feel that here and now we should give the native pony his due, because at Burley are held his races, gymkhana, and show. Of course there are many poor specimens to be seen wandering over the Forest, and even a first-rate pony will look a bit of a wreck with half-cast coat, staring ribs, and ragged hips. To judge him fairly you should go to the shows at Lyndhurst and Burley, where you will discover that the best the Forest can produce is equal to the best in these islands, and so in the world.

Our pony is not descended, as some say, from Spanish horses who swam ashore from one of the Great Armada's wrecked galleons. He comes direct from the courageous little beasts who drew the scythe-wheeled war-chariots into battle in the days of wolves and woad. Then in the eighteenth and nineteenth centuries people of wisdom and experience began to spend money on improving him. It is said that Marske, sire of the famous Eclipse, was sent here by the Duke of Northumberland; it is known that Queen Victoria's Arab stallion Zorab stood at New Park from 1852 to 1860. At different periods more Arabs and excellent little stallions from the Devon moors, the fells of Cumberland, the Scottish Highlands, Ireland, and the Welsh mountains were drafted into the New Forest. Our pony assimilated them all, the bitter winters weeded out those of poor stamina, and he became the gallant handsome fellow he is to-day.

I owe Bill many good things, but the most pleasant of them all is the friendship of Mr. Bramble, the breeder of the best strain in the Forest to-day, and an acknowledged judge and expert. Bill cut his foot; the new doctor, seeing him parading Ringwood in an amateurish bandage, offered with characteristic kindness to sew the wound up. During the operation his pretty young wife came in and helped hold down the patient, who was really trying to be brave. We became great friends, and then one day they took me to Avon Farm, where Mr. and Mrs. John Bramble live, loved and respected by all their acquaintance in the Forest. Dazzled by the dining room's display of challenge cups, medals, and much fine silver won in the show-ring

by his ponies, I asked Mr. Bramble which of the animals
he had bred he considered to be the best. ' Labby Loo,'
he said, and showed me the photograph of the handsome
little beast in George Tweedie's *Hampshire's Glorious
Wilderness*. Then he took me out to a wide field where
some young stallions sent by their owner to winter under
his expert care were playing about. They were like little
Velasquez chargers, with bright intelligent eyes, neat
heads, curving crests, powerful quarters, good shoulders
and excellent legs. Racing, wheeling, rearing high up,
lashing out with wicked heels they had the appearance of
savages difficult to deal with. Shortly after I saw them
walking round the show-ring in hemp-halters only, behaving like perfect gentlemen. They left the ring a
smother of winning ribbons, the champion among them.

Before leaving a subject so dear to our hearts we will
set down the exploits of two mares, so that there may be
no doubt about the capabilities of a really first-rate Forest
pony.

' Squib,' foaled in 1814 and only twelve hands high,
trotted three miles in eight minutes, and took only one
hour and a quarter to cover twenty miles of the country
between Egham and Farnham. The other mare, bred in
the 'eighties, had an unbeaten racing career. It is recorded that on one occasion she was driven six miles to
the racecourse, was entered for three races in succession,
which entailed the running of six heats, won the lot, and
then trotted the six miles home as perky as you please.

What Gervase Markham said of the Irish hobby is true
of our ponies to-day, ' sure of foot, and nimble in dan-

gerous places, and of lively courage, tough in travel . . .,'
and, we can add, of kind temper and pleasant manners.

We had mapped out a route covering ten miles for our
first Burley walk, eight miles of which lay through the
woods. It proved a grand example of what a woodland
walk in the New Forest may bring the follower of ride and
track, so we have set it down here in detail.

A lane leaves the village main road at the 'Queen's Head,'
crosses two springs and forks shortly afterwards. The
left fork goes back to Burley Moor and joins the main
road again at Burley Street; the right fork runs on between woods, past Burley Lodge, over Blackwater, and
joins the Lyndhurst highway between Dames Slough and
Knightwood Enclosures.

We went down this road early one glorious April
morning, took the right fork and followed it until we came
to the gorsey green on the left, which is spread before the
beginning of the main army of the 'middle area's'
woods. This was Oakley Enclosure, and leaving the road
we entered it by a gate near one of the many springs which
go to the making of Oberwater.

In ancient days there were potteries here instead of trees,
and the wood was not planted until 1853. Scots pine and
oak were set first, and then, much later, an avenue of
Douglas firs which, with characteristic push, have entirely
outgrown their elders.

We had under our feet the main track, gravelled, wide
and faultless. It is popular with saddle folk, of whom we
kept meeting happy little groups mounted on admirable
specimens of the native pony, looking very business-like

with their close-clipped, satiny coats, neatly ' tucked ' long tails, and maneless necks.

About half a mile of walking took us past the gravel track to ' Old House,' where a generous-hearted writer, Auberon Herbert, used to live. His kindness took many forms it seems, but one hears mostly about the huge free teas he gave, welcoming all and sundry no matter who they might be. The house is on the edge of Oakley, facing Backley Plain and neighboured by a little wood rejoicing in the fairy tale name of Mouse's Cupboard.

A tributary of Blackwater goes under the main track some way above the Old House turning, and a mile above the stream we came to a fork. The left fork goes to the Ringwood highway past Bratley Wood, the right one, after clinging to Oakley for yet another mile, scales a moorland slope and comes out on top of Mogshade Hill. Bratley Water and another little stream meet near the fork on their way to fill Burley Lodge pond, and above their meeting place is a ride that skirts Anderwood and goes on to Mark Ash.

We continued some way along the right fork till we arrived at a ride on the right, and decided to take it, realising that the flow of pony parties would have scared away the wild things we had hoped to see from the vicinity of the main track. It was a blessed choice.

Almost at once, directly we had stepped across the stream, we felt quite alone and at peace. Dew still hung on the grass blades and brambles, because the trees grew so thickly that their branches wove a dense shield against the sun. The ground, mounting in a series of quite big

105

ups and downs, showed brown with pine needles and
streaked with slender bars of sunlight between the close
packed trunks. In this mysterious, silent, dusky part of
the wood we felt something really worth while might
happen, nor were we mistaken.

A swift pattering on the dead leaves drew my attention
to Bill. He was circling, alert and tense, under the trees
in a manner Mr. Bundy and I had learned to know and
welcome as a sure omen of good fun to come. He disappeared swiftly over a knoll, and we, tingling with excitement, continued our way, making such efforts to keep a
lookout on every side at once that it is a marvel we did not
contract squints. Every now and then we caught sight
of a flying white form racing along, nose to ground, at ever
increasing speed. We knew the quarry was near at hand,
but we did not see it until we reached the gate opening on
to the first green slopes of Mark Ash.

Mark Ash is one of the most famous woods in the
Forest, and though we had been thrilled by the thought
that to-day we were to see it we had not guessed what a
wonderful meeting it was to be.

At the gate Bill was very near to us, but too intent on the
heady scent to see the vision vouchsafed Mr. Bundy and
me. Quite unalarmed by the white hunter they knew to
be no match for their arrowy speed and woodland lore,
two deer went in graceful, leisurely leaps back along the
trail up which poor Bill had so painstakingly followed
them, stopping occasionally to watch him working feverishly beyond the rails in Mark Ash. Their coats were
neither grey nor spotted, but a rich, dark dun against

106

which their raised tails fanned out whitely. They looked very beautiful stealing away through the gloomy pine trunks, now shadowy as a myth, now brightly barred with gold as they passed through the shafts of sunlight.

As we stood watching them fade, a poignant, heart-searching cry fell suddenly from the sky. We looked up and to our amazement and delight saw, planeing in the narrow airway visible between the branches, a knightly form. Though we loved the trees for showing us the deer, at that moment we could have seen them felled without a qualm, for now they were preventing us from watching the flight of one of nature's most superb air aces, the buzzard. The bird was soon joined by his mate, and for a few dazzling seconds they played together; then, calling mellifluously to him, she led him out of our ken.

Delighted by what we had just seen we went through the gate and started to climb up among Mark Ash's beeches, feeling the day had done more than well by us and that we really could not expect it to do any more. But this morning we were to live our crowded hour of glorious life.

Bill, earnestly questing, was off again, but as we thought he was only hunting the old line we were completely taken by surprise when a quick movement against some hollies discovered a small herd of deer affrightedly gazing at us. Unprepared, we committed the grand error of stopping dead. Away they went like lightning, snaking in and out through the trunks of hollies and beeches with such bewildering pace that they were swallowed up before we had quite taken in what we had seen, or had time to count them.

For the rest of the way we kept losing Bill, but we saw no more deer. We found the track we were aiming for, metalled like a road, which winds down from Boldrewood Green through Boldrewood Grounds, Mark Ash and Knightwood Enclosures to the Lyndhurst highway. We joined it just below Boldrewood Lodge, a cottage standing near the site of a house where a lordly person called a ' master-keeper ' lived prior to 1833. The master-keeper received no salary and his work was done by ' groom-keepers.' The big house, occupied by Lord Delaware in 1732, was enlarged in 1747, and pulled down in 1833. On the south side of the cottage are two oaks, nearly choked by the saplings and brambles growing within the rails put up to protect them. Each has a stone saying why it was planted : the one commemorates the corona-tion of King Edward the Seventh, the other that of King George the Fifth.

Turning right we went down the track and were soon under some of the finest beeches in the Forest. It is curious how beeches can vary. Until we got to know the old woods of the Forest we thought of a beech as a stately tree, with lofty pewter trunk, a beautiful spread of bran-ches, and a canopy of sunlit green leaves. To think of it in any other way seemed an insult. Now we know that a beech, though it may soar to almost any height, may also sink to almost any depth. Mark Ash has examples of this sad truth. There are two trees, not out of the way in size but of the most exquisite growth, at the side of the track about half-way down the hill on a sharp bend. The trunk of one of them sweeps up from the ground in folds like drapery ; that of the other might have given the Normans the idea for those clustered shafts they so frequently made the bearers of arcade and chancel arch. All round them are big, burly, pollarded fellows whose grand air of strength makes up for their lack of elegance. But leave the track and wander about a bit and you will soon discover among much splendid growth the kind of skeletons that nearly every beech wood keeps in its cupboard. Squat, distorted, and warty, they give one a feeling of watchfulness, as though witches and hobgoblins had for a moment taken on tree shapes to further their evil ends. Stand still when you meet such a group and you will learn that they speak to each other in a secret code of squeaks, groans and cracks, though no wind is aloft to help the branches send their messages. That a beech can be as treacherous as the much abused elm I can bear witness, for once when I was riding past a hill-top beech cover in Wiltshire the still air was suddenly split by a fiendish screeching and roaring as one of the great trees crashed to the ground behind me.

There are only a few ugly trees in Mark Ash, and very many majestic ones, among them the 'Queen Beech,' which measures over eighteen feet round.

A gate let us into Knightwood Enclosure, planted in 1867 but mostly cut down during the War. However, a host of pines and oaks and beeches have survived, and the lumbermen still find plenty of material for their axes. We passed some of these men loading newly barked pine trunks on to waggons, called carriages here, helped by obedient great horses. One man had a good-looking pony stallion to haul the logs into position. The little beast was working as eagerly and intelligently as a sheep dog, his only headgear a bitless halter.

Just short of the Enclosure's Lyndhurst highway gate, on the left of the track, grows the ' Knightwood Oak,' a tree whose renown as one of the Forest ' sights ' is widespread. He is approached with due pomp ; an avenue of courtly beeches lead to his throne, others are grouped in a respectful circle round him, and at the beginning of the avenue is a sentinel clump of the same trees. Though pollarded in his youth the giant is an impressive sight, with his great girth of over twenty-one feet and his huge branches thrusting fiercely up like a young forest.

Cars whizz along the Lyndhurst highway with even greater velocity than on the Ringwood road, for its surface is perfect and cries out for speed. Out of Knightwood, and turning right, we only had a short half-mile to go before we reached the haven of Dames Slough Enclosure, but on that perilous highway it seemed to Mr. Bundy and me a league at least. With a sigh of relief we gained the pleasant wood and followed the ride for another half mile. Then we took to another ride which went over a small stream and followed this new path until we came to its meeting with the ride from Burley road. We went up the ride right-handed and soon found ourselves out on the road between Burley Lodge and its pond.

The ' Twelve Apostle Oaks ' used to grow at the lodge, but their glory has long ago departed and most of them have fallen down. The pond can easily be seen through the hedge, and the stream which feeds it comes tumbling down some falls, glitters across the road under a white timber bridge and disappears into Dames Slough, where it eventually becomes the Blackwater.

A groom on a chestnut pony which was apparently endeavouring to do the rhumba were occupying the road when we got there. The young man's skill and patience filled us with such admiration that we stopped to watch. After a bit it struck me that the pony was frightened to pass a fallen bough on the roadside, so I offered to lead it by. The weary rider said the pony was not frightened but ' nappy,' that its mother had been nappy too, and a nappy horse was incurable. Having never met a really horrid native pony before, we waited to see what sort of a fight a real bad lot can put up. The red pony wanted to go home, its rider wanted to go on, so it took him into thorn bushes and tried to rub his leg against a railing in the hope that such tactics would make him change his mind. If its rider tried backing it his mount got up on its hind legs at once. We realised that the tussle was to be a longer one than we had thought, and that if we waited for the end we should be late for lunch, an awful disaster in Bill's mind, so we went on. When we came to a bend in the road a quarter of a mile farther up we looked back at the combatants and saw them hard at it still.

II

A longer, equally beautiful walk, and one offering as many chances as that we followed on our first venture from Burley, is to go up the main track through Oakley, and a little over two miles up take a ride branching off to the right. When you get into the main Boldrewood-Mark Ash-Knightwood track turn left and it will bring you through an avenue of splendid Douglas firs, whose branches droop downwards like the folded tails of peacocks, on to Boldrewood Green. Here are usually two or three motor-cars and picnic parties.

The track bears left through gorse and hollies along the top of Mogshade Hill, 343 feet up. Ahead, across Bratley Wood and Slufter's Enclosure, rise the first of the lofty northern plains ; on the right is Holmhill or Highland Water Enclosure and Stony Cross. The road you cross to reach Holmhill comes up from the Ringwood highway, and after a brief passage over Mogshade's bare poll the rest of its journey is a gradual descent through woods to Emery Down and Lyndhurst.

Just across the road is a gate in an iron band fence. From this gate you look out over the deep, steep-sided valley, part moor, part wood, that is Holmhill Enclosure, across the southerly woods of the Forest, to Spithead and the curving chalk downs of the Isle of Wight. As soon as you can tear yourself away from this invigorating sight go through the gate and follow the track down the thickly heathered, baby-pine sown hillside, over Highland Water, here at the nursery stage and hiding under sprawling, untidy young oaks, up the opposite slope to beechen Puckpits which occupies the north-east corner of the enclosure.

We had a sunny, windless day in April, perfect for birds and the earlier butterflies, when we first came this way. Stonechats, exquisite little fellows like clerical redbreasts with their round white collars and dark jackets, were jigging up and down on the unsteadiest of gorse tops and chit-chatting away at us for all they were worth ; finches and yellow-hammers were filling the trees with the ' mirth of their mouths,' larks were shrilling energetically in the clouds. As for sulphur butterflies, they seemed to be everywhere.

For the first few yards of the hill up to Puckpits oaks and pines dispute every foot of the way, but the usurping pines soon beat back the oaks and for a while have it all their own way. The pines are the master trees of Holmhill, crowning the valley tops, climbing down the slopes, filing across the boggy bottom and arrogantly shouldering the few oaks and beeches that get in their path.

But with Puckpits it is different. The old wood refuses to bow to the pushing conifers, and resolute as a die-hard Tory he snubs their every advance. To begin with he draws an arbitrary line in the shape of a bank across the track and then stations a policeman oak upon it. The oak is an oddity: springing up from the ground in four separate trunks like a starfish he is obviously and rather theatrically waving back the sullen pines.

Beyond the bank the change is immediate and most welcome. Instead of coarse grass, spiny bramble and dead bracken, there is laid at the feet of the trees a green

H

and golden pavement of whortleberry and beech leaves. Instead of dusty, untidy trunked pines and starveling oaks, bickering and shouldering each other, the satin, knightly boles of breeches stand about with an easy dignity. A spacious, airy wood, and on the day we first came to it vibrant with the deep love croonings of the grey pigeons. A wren, too, suddenly struck up with piercing sweetness from a big tree, drowning the pigeons and making the wood resound with his voice. We never hear it without amazement ; the bird is so minute, his song so much too big for him, and yet he manages it with such exhilarating ease that he has made it one of the most glorious achievements in the bird world of music.

At the top of the wood the track is joined by another one, and just beyond this second footway the ground drops sheer. The hollow is choked with larches and black as night. While we were peering into it a tall young woodsman came along, his native grace of movement quelling his horrid blue serge suit, an axe at his thigh. He knew all about this part of the Forest, told us that the gloomy pit below was called Dark Hole, and that it grew the best larch timber this side of Lyndhurst. As an instance he gave the measurements of a tree felled the day before which throughout a length of eighty-five feet had a diameter of eight inches. I asked him what was done with the bark, and he said it was always burnt as it harboured the weevil, which breeds fast and will spread quickly to the growing trees after it has consumed the stripped bark left lying about.

We left Puckpits by Pound Hill Gate, so called because

of the small oak-railed pen beside it where colts are 'pounded, and came out on to the heather above Withybed Bottom. The hills look lovely from here. Back on the left is the pine-maned slope of Holmhill and heathy Mogshade Hill; on the right the severe line of Stony Cross and the sharp trees of the Grove; in the middle, the fine height topped by Ocknell Plain, with Ocknell Enclosure and the neighbouring beech copse our woodsman told us was called Winding Stonehard upon its slopes. Near Winding Stonehard is a notable roadside oak, its great limbs a-sprawl, called Spread Oak.

Approaching us over the moor there appeared a wonderful being, all Adam's apple, horn-rims, and knees. It wore shorts, a ' Shelley ' shirt, and toyed with a knobbly ash stick. When Bill saw it he rushed towards it barking hilariously, to the great discomfort of the poor hiker, who left the track at high speed and bounded away across the heather with surprising agility, his pack dealing him sounding thwacks behind at every leap. I got hold of Bill and called to the flying hiker that all was well, but he continued his course, and if he did not get bogged in the Bottom must have set up a new record for the mile by the time he gained Mogshade Hill. It was all very sad, and curious too, because Bill is almost too friendly as a rule, and had rather sickened Mr. Bundy and me by his fawnings upon the woodsman. We can only put his lapse down to an undue sensitiveness where clothes are concerned.

At the gate we turned right and followed the track close to the woods, went under some beeches, and when we came to where it drops down between some gorse bushes, left it for a moment for the sake of the heavenly glimpse our woodsman had told us we should get over the enclosure gate. Through an avenue of tall larches, across miles of undulating valley woods, we saw the strong curves of the Island blue-green in the distance. The avenue was alive with sulphur butterflies.

The going is good as long as it keeps near the wood, but directly it turns away and begins to descend to a heath, with a gravel pit and a biggish house at the far end, it develops a nasty boggy patch into which Bill went up to his tummy, emerging with black boots and yellow waistcoat. Mr. Bundy and I, disliking mud at any time and bog mud in particular, went over the heather above it and got down to the heath dryshod.

Many dogs dwell in the house at the heath's end, and among them is one peppery old gentleman who foolishly thought it his duty to tackle Bill, with the result that he was on his back in a flash with three stone of bull terrier sitting on his chest. It was the groom who helped me remove Bill who told us that the hill marked on our map as Pilmore Gate Heath is known locally as Acres Down. So if you are afflicted with a map like ours (a document only a little more reliable than that of the Conqueror's monkish biographers) cross out the former name and write in its stead Acres Down. The groom also told us that five bucks had been grazing outside the house early that morning.

Our heads were so full of this thrilling information that we overshot the track up to Acres Down, a gravel path hedged with hollies on our right, and were soon threading our way to a small farm down a green path strewn with vast recumbent pigs and bony, friendly sheepdogs, with wall eyes and matted coats horribly suggestive of over-population. The owner of this charming family told us that if, when we got to the wood just ahead, we turned right and scaled the hill, bearing right on reaching the top we should get into the track we wanted.

Up we went and found ourselves on a little hill-top heath commanding marvellous views over the Forest to the Island. When the track forked we went right, as we were aiming at the delightfully named Holiday Hill Enclosure ; a left turn would have taken us to red brick Emery Down.

A big clump of hollies stand over the track we took, and into it shot Mr. Bundy and Bill as if they had been propelled by the selfsame catapult. I heard the deer go away, but, alack ! the cover was too dense for me to see them, and my part of the fun was a weary wait for the return of the hunters.

When they came back we proceeded across the heath, admiring the beautiful beeches growing outside Holmhill's railings in the bottom on our right. They are marked on our map as Wood Crates, but no one we met had ever heard of them being so called.

Still bearing right we went down the slope of Acres Down and were soon among the beeches. We found them to be big fellows, some well grown, some covered with blains, others suffering from ingrowth. A dark slender girl in a primrose shirt, faultless breeches and boots, came riding through the trees on a chestnut filly, young and graceful as herself. She told us how to go, and after I had extracted Bill from under the filly, in whose shelter he had been hobnobbing with the black and golden cockers accompanying their young mistress, she cantered off, the most charming thing we had seen that day.

All we had to do was to keep straight on down the path, for it went quickly to a gate into Holmhill. We went up the ride beyond it for a while, crossed a gutter and turning left went over Highland Water, and after a climb, typical of Holmhill, with its clearings, pine clumps, falls and rises, came out through a splendid assemblage of beeches on to the Mogshade-Emery Down road at Woosen's Hill.

Nearly opposite us was the gate into Holiday Hill for which we had been hoping. The enclosure is poor in adult trees but a very mother-of-thousands where baby beeches, oaks, and larches are concerned ; most of them we think are self-sown with the exception of the larches. We left the gravel track almost at once, that is, as soon as we saw a green ride on the right, and went pleasantly down it, passing an occasional batch of full-grown larches, until we came to a gate into Knightwood. Immediately beyond the gate the big trees begin. First come stalwart beeches, among them one with so many trunks that it has the appearance of a Victorian family waiting for the private bus which is to take them on the first stages of their seaside holiday. Then mighty pines tower above the beeches in the dusky avenue beginning on the other side the stream which comes quietly out of the wood, slips across the ride and disappears as quickly as possible among the trees again.

At the avenue's end is the main Knightwood track, and we came out on to it just above the ' Knightwood Oak.' A bit higher up we turned into a wide grass drive running through pine trees and over clearings to the Burley Lodge road. Near the gate into the road this drive is joined by another in which, no distance up, is the ' Eagle Oak,' a rather bedraggled old fellow suggesting that the moulting season was upon its noble namesake, and half smothered by a motherly yew who spreads her skirts to cover his nakedness. An eagle was shot in its branches in the late nineteenth century, hence its name.

There are rides in plenty through Dames Slough to the moor beyond Burley New Enclosure, and in every one of them will be found in April some springtime act of grace. Against the velvet darkness of pines the delicate green smoke of young birches will suddenly trail, or there will be a brief snow-shower of thorn blossom ; celandines and violets start up unexpectedly on the banks of a stream, or a pallid primrose peers from the shadow of a fiery tuft of gorse. The ride we love best is easy to find, because all you have to do is to go right-handed up the road on leaving Knightwood, and when you get to the top of the sharp little hill go through the gate on your left. Take the first ride on your right and then the first on the left. Thus it was we came to where the Blackwater crosses the way in delightful fashion between golden and purple flowered banks, honey-scented gorse, cool pines, and frosty thorn bushes. Under the plank bridge the water had delved a deep hole and filled it to the brim so that one can swim a lazy stroke or so without barking one's knees on the gravel bed.

We had just left the clearing beyond the Blackwater and had gained the trees of Burley New Enclosure when a care-free crackling of brushwood made us look back. A brave sight met our eyes—fortunately only those of Mr. Bundy and myself, Bill being a long way ahead. Two bucks were cantering up behind us in single file, a little to the right, leaping over the brambles of the clearing with no attempt at concealment or quietness. A superhuman effort enabled us to go steadily on. Catching our feet in the trailing brambles and stumbling over the ruts and ridges of the track we went, our heads screwed round to keep the exquisite animals in view.

One buck crossed an intersecting ride and was under the trees and level with us before he realised we were there. Then he stopped, pointing his shiny black muzzle at us, tilting his graceful antlers back as he raised his head to watch us with calm, almond-shaped eyes, confident that we had seen nothing. His friend remained in the bleached, tumbled growth of the clearing, matching it to perfection, his antlers looking like the dry branches of a little dead tree. When they judged that we had gone far enough from them to make swift movement safe they wheeled as at a word of command and fled away, back over the clearing, twisting and turning with incredible agility down the hidden deer-paths, leaping over the sharper corners and disappearing completely, long before they reached the trees, after the magic manner of their kind.

120

We never felt more like laughter when on turning we saw Bill waiting for us in the distance, a bored smile of pity for our dawdling progress upon his fat face, and knew him to be quite unaware of what had happened.

A little over half a mile from the stream we turned left and soon came out of the enclosure. Bearing left we went through a scattering of low oaks, beeches, hollies, and thorns, over Ober Water by a narrow timber bridge, and up the moor into the pleasant road winding round Bisterne Closes, skirting the golf links, and ending in the main road by the school.

CHAPTER VIII

WOODS, BOGS AND
HEATHS

WE purposely refrained from describing the Bisterne Closes road and the moor descending from it to the two Burley enclosures because we feel that they, being so beautiful, should come at the beginning not the end of a walk.

Oaks, beeches, and hollies avenue the road nearly the whole way from the links to the moor. Few things, to our minds, are more pleasant than walking in the cool shade of handsome trees and looking past their trunks at miles of moors and distant woods quivering under a blazing sun. The trees give way occasionally; once to let the tarmac road to Holmesley station go by, and once to allow the sun to fill the gardens and bake the thatch of some cottages. In the fields belonging to these dwellings saddle ponies idle under trees or graze industriously among the little jumps over which they take the embryo horseman.

But for the rest of the way the green awning is unbroken, though houses, redolent of the suburbs, line one side of it. Each house has something nice to make up for the bricks which will not grow old gracefully and the paint that is either too loudly white, or too dismally grey. One has a field full of dear comfortable honey-coloured hens; another is hidden under cherry blossom; a third has a most engaging family of dachshunds. We have a great weakness for dachshunds, and know a brown one called Max whose bosom friend is a Siamese cat. Their games together are the delight of their acquaintance, but they are most taking when they go to sleep on their communal

124

cushion and Max puts his podgy front paws round the neck of the cat snuggling as close as she can under his chin.

By the house with the dachshunds the road curves on its way round the back of the Closes. At this bend there is a path that strikes out through the trees on to the moor. It runs downhill, enters a group of old holly trees, and when it comes out presents the walker with an amazingly lovely view. The rich motley moor drops sharply from the hollies to Mill Lawn, a pale green strip where, curtained by thorns and low-growing oaks, the Ober Water dawdles along under the name of Mill Lawn Brook. Beyond, as far as eye can see, stretch the woods which fill the country between Picket Post and Brockenhurst. The land climbs steadily from the stream's banks to Mogshade Hill, a mellow tapestry of greens, browns, and purples in spring, and of every variety of green in summer. As with everything else in this world these miles of woodland are most enchanting early in the year. Then the dark, sharp shapes of the pines are accentuated by the gossamer green of the birches ; the strident note of the young larches, the Fascists among trees, is tactfully handled by the plum-bloomed, russet tolerance of the old, experienced beeches still in the throes of cracking the hard cases of their latest buds. The oak, a martial tree, garbs his branches in khaki when the year is young, and marching through the woods, his sober-hued battalions soothe and steady the different colours, persuading them to conform to the peaceful law of harmony.

It was at Mill Lawn that we saw our first Forest curlew. We had left the path because it chooses a rather bare,

uninteresting place in which to cross the water, and had
gone up the low bank to where the oaks and white blossomed thorns begin. Here we sat down awhile to watch
the minnows, each with a neat black water-line along his
hull, rubbing lazily against the green water plants, untroubled by the absurd, Micky Mouse-like shadows,
which, ringed with light, scampered over the stream's bed
and belonged to the giant water flies skating about on the
surface. The curlew's voice sounding far away brought
us with a rush to our feet. Running out of the trees in the
hope that the bird might be coming our way we looked up
into the cloudless sky, and guided by the clear, bubbling
cry we saw him flying steadily towards the north, a sturdy
shape with sunlit breast and dark wings. He was too far
off for us to see his long, curved bill. It is queer how many
of the more elegant birds which haunt rivers have something akin to the sounds of water in their calls. The
curlew and redshank particularly possess a rippling note
which seems as if it must have been suggested to them
by some tiny waterfall on the moors.

A single balk of timber, just wide enough for Mr.
Bundy's nervous passage, is the only means of getting dryshod over the stream ; fortunately it is provided with a
handrail. A wide, soft track, hedged by hollies, thorns, a
few oaks and silver birches, begins on the other side.
Under the grass is clay, so the track is nearly always wet.
Soon it forks ; the left branch with a dead oak in it is the
one by which we came out of Burley New the day we saw
the two bucks ; the other goes under stout oaks, knotty
beeches, and hollies to Burley Old Enclosure.

126

On entering the wood if, as we did, you want to go as straight as possible to Knightwood, you must keep along with the track, and not leave it as we did for the seductive little path branching off on the right. The path eventually arrives at a gate on the Lyndhurst highway, making it necessary either to turn left and follow a ride till you get to another on the right, or to go straight ahead by almost invisible paths made by deer and rabbits until you come into a ride near another gate facing the Lyndhurst road, with a pound near it. Turn your back on the gate, go up the ride and you will soon come to where it is crossed by a second one, down which you must turn right-handed and it will bring you out opposite Knightwood Enclosure.

Burley Old was planted by William IV to provide timber for his ships, so it is almost entirely an oak wood, and as such is friendly to ferns, grasses, and wildflowers as well as to birds and animals. Bill had a wild chase after a rabbit here. It had seen us coming and had retired into temporary cover under a mound of brambles. But its scent was too strong for it to escape the notice of Mr. Bundy's unerring nose, and Bill, seeing his friend busily poking at the brambles, came racing back and proceeded to jump up and down on them till the rabbit bolted. Needless to say it soon gave Bill the slip by the simple ruse of diving into just such another lot of brambles, but that poor simpleton continued to tear round in huge circles looking for the rabbit, which he passed at every round, clearing its hiding place whenever he came to it until he was too blown to go on.

Out of Burley Old the way lies through Knightwood, over the Lyndhurst highway by the 'Knightwood Oak,' and through the grand beeches of Vinney Ridge where once there was a heronry, which now, alas! is no more. Here the track is a gravel road down which cars are allowed to crawl, but in early spring there are not many there.

The beeches give way all too soon and are succeeded by rhododendrons and enormous Douglas firs. The road is here stricken with the name of 'the Ornamental Drive,' as though it belonged to some fearful seaside resort instead of to the woods and moors of Rhinefield Walk. The dogs do not share my distaste for rhododendrons, but welcome them as affording wonderful games of hide-and-seek. Once a fox played this game with them right from the beginning of the Drive up to where the wide and shallow Blackwater drifts across the road. The clever creature never showed himself to me, and but for his taint lying strong on the air I should not have known what it was that was leading the dogs such a dance and making them so excited.

The enclosure comes to an end soon after the stream appears, beyond the gate comes a brief bit of heath, and then grass and woods line the road. There are two cottages on the right, one of them at the drive gate of Rhinefield Lodge, which is the big stone house looking over the fence a little farther on.

From this point there are several things one can do besides going straight on over the moor to Brockenhurst; here are three that we did.

A Stream near Brockenhurst

I

When the private oak pailings belonging to Rhinefield Lodge came to an end we took the second gate into Clumber Enclosure, a pleasant wood of oaks and sweet chestnuts, and went along the rather spongy ride ahead of us. A broad drive cuts across it when it passes behind Rhinefield Lodge, the trees having been cleared away so that the house has an uninterrupted view over moorland hills to Wilverley Enclosure.

Our ride got sounder when near the end of the wood, the change being due to pine trees whose roots hold the ground together and fill up any crevices with springy needles and hard cones. Under the pines the ride dropped down to a gate and came out on to a heathy bottom framed by gentle pine tree covered hills and threaded by Ober Water.

By the timber bridge are pools big enough for total immersion, and which, we thought, would be excellent dozing places for trout. But though we looked long and patiently we saw nothing except black and gold pebbles, and the fretful water weeds they clutched by the roots. That there are plenty of trout in the Forest's streams we know, but we have never seen anything bigger than a minnow ourselves. Our bad luck greatly amuses some young friends of ours, who catch quite a lot in a prehistoric but highly successful manner. These boys, the sons of farm labourers, stroll along a stream peering into the shadows under overhanging banks until they see a fish worthy of the name. Then with swift, unerring aim they spear it with their home-made harpoons—ordinary kitchen forks lashed to light bamboo canes.

From the stream the track goes up through an oblong wood of pines and oaks called Ferney Knap Enclosure, over a short stretch of heath, and ends at the Lyndhurst highway. We turned up Markway Hill when we got to the tarmac, showing as cool a front to the traffic as we could muster, and, taking the first track we came to on the right, got back to the Bisterne Closes road across the heather.

II

The second time we came down through Vinney Ridge we went on past Clumber Enclosure and followed the road along by Aldridge Enclosure, over the Ober Water by Puttles Bridge and on to the moor. At the top of the rise above the brook the first houses of Brockenhurst appear in the distance, and little over half a mile from Puttles Bridge a track runs off to the left, heading towards a red house and the trees of Beechern Wood.

The distance from the moor road to Boldresford Bridge for which we were steering is not great—perhaps a mile and a half, but it is both charming and varied.

It was a mild morning in spring when we first came along the track to Beechern Wood and a fine rain was still falling after a night of drizzle. Wetness had brought out the warm smell of peat, gorse, and heather, and so strengthened the rich hues of the moor that it had gained as much in appearance as a parti-coloured pebble does when dropped into clear water. The woods on our left and ahead looked purple and the fields near Brockenhurst almost brazenly green against the indigo hills beyond. Beautiful as it was the bosky stretch beyond the red house of Beechern Wood surpassed it.

On one side of the track were a few fields framed by low hedges on whose banks grew, among the big soft-leaved young foxgloves, a host of wild violets and little white wood sorrel. The other side was lovelier still. Beyond the big oaks under which we walked, in a setting of pale young willow leaves and made bright by rain, powdery white thorn blossom and brilliant gorse bloom rioted above the ruddy bracken and sweet gale massed at their feet. Here Ober Water draws near, and soon a track from Aldridge crossed it and joined ours. We were glad when we got to the bridge that we had stepped aside to pay it a visit, because of the glimpse it gave us of the peaty bubble-ridden stream brushing past banks laden with sweet gale and pored over by willows, thorns, and gorse.

When the fields end a low green hill covered with trees begins, and then comes Black Knowl Heath.

On that moist morning we found the heath a golden tide of gorse, gorgeous under a dove-coloured sky and surrounded by misty woods. We had heard a cuckoo calling as we walked through Beechern Wood, and now as we came out on to the heath we saw the hawk-like bird. There was something of urgency in her flight and we thought as we watched her that nothing short of a gunshot could stop or turn her. But we were wrong. As she approached the trees on which she had set her heart a swarm of little birds rushed out to do battle, attacking so determinedly that after ducking and feinting in fruitless efforts to get past them the cuckoo had to turn tail.

Having shaken off the hunt the poor bird began calling mournfully from the woods into which she had escaped, and almost at once a watery ray of sun came out and a flight of swallows skimmed by, darting and diving like a school of heavenly fish. Then we felt that the times were almost as rich and rare as they were when sun and rain composed such a marvellous accompaniment for the song of Davies' cuckoo.

We have felt acutely sorry for the cuckoo ever since someone, I forget who, told us that she is not really the heartless society mama we had thought her, whose one idea is to shift the responsibility of her child's upbringing on to somebody else's shoulders. She is really a devoted mother, afflicted by Nature with so curved a breastbone that she cannot sit upon an egg without bursting it. Far from being callous about her offspring's fate she makes its welfare her chief concern, searching feverishly for the ideal nursery and foster-mother. It is usually a pipit on whom she confers the honour of bringing up her chick, and the nest she chooses is one containing a single egg only. Her reasons for selecting an almost empty nest being that if there is a full clutch the hen will have been sitting for several days already and will hatch her own chicks out first and so not give the foster egg its proper amount of incubation. On the other hand, if there are no eggs in the nest, it is probable that the pipits will desert a home which apparently provides its own eggs before they have had time to begin their own family.

132

From the various books at my disposal I gather that, though the small birds will fight bravely to defend their nest against the full-grown cuckoo, they feel no animosity for her young, either as an egg or as a fledgeling. One authority says that he has even seen a baby cuckoo sitting on the grass and being waited on by several different pairs of little birds, only one of which could have had the rearing of it. Hudson has watched a pair of robins plying back and forth all day with grubs and flies for the young cuckoo in their nest, while the last of their own brood lay close by on a bright green dockleaf where they could not have failed to see it, dying and neglected while they fed the little wretch who had hoisted it overboard.

Boldreford Bridge stands at the meeting of Ober Water with Highland Water as if it were a parson and they were bride and bridegroom. After the ceremony the happy pair proceed to the sea as the Lymington River. Their honeymoon is spent in Waterford Copse, the long narrow wood running into Buckford Enclosure, which is opposite the Balmer Lawn hotel in Brockenhurst. It is an enchanting wood in spring because violets, windflowers, primroses and wood sorrel grow under the trees, and kingcups gild the water's edge. Once when walking here I had occasion to call Bill's attention by cracking the whip, whereupon a heron, up till then hidden from me by the bank of the stream, rose majestically and flew up its course without disturbing a twig of the overhanging bushes in spite of his mighty wing spread.

In front of Boldreford Bridge (Waterford Copse is on the right as you come from Beechern Wood) lies the private road to New Park, and on the left is the track to Queen Bower. The worst of Queen Bower is that it happens to be a popular ' beauty spot,' further cursed by ease of access. Each time we have come here we have been unlucky ; first we found Easter campers indulging in awkward antics with balls and giving vent to noises like those which float down to Regent's Park from the Mappin terraces ; next time we came upon unlimited gramophone-accompanied picnic parties ; and another time found the ground littered with the refuse left by others of the same kidney.

Therefore nowadays we keep sternly to the track, which goes along by the side of Highland Water, under fine oaks and beeches among which are two dead trees drilled full of holes by woodpeckers. On one tree is an ancient notice saying ' No Sugaring ' ; it is here for the protection of butterflies, of which there are rare and lovely specimens in the Forest.

Track and stream keep on together through the pines, birches, and thorn bushes beyond the Bower, with woods and a few fields on one hand and shaggy Poundhill Heath backed by its enclosure on the other, until a second bridge, more humble than Boldreford Bridge and unnamed, crosses the stream and ushers one into the outskirts of Brinken Wood.

Here, on our first visit, we paused completely flum-, moxed, gazing from our map, which showed a single, well-defined path running straight through the wood, to the many hairy paths disappearing in the thicket most unhelpfully confronting us. After a bit we decided to cast forward, keeping as near as possible straight on but with a leaning to the right. This turned out to be the correct move, for after passing a long smear of stagnant water on the left we again came up with Highland Water. Led by our charming guide we went under splendid beeches by mossy and russet paths where violets grew in generous batches, their colour marvellously intensified by the red brown drifts of leaves through which they had thrust themselves, until at last we reached the Lyndhurst highway just above a bridge and a cottage whose garden was full of the snowdrop's big cousin, the snowflake.

Over the highway a gravel track mounts sturdily up a beech-covered hill, and this we took, for after a pleasant journey it enters Holidays Hill Enclosure, and from Holidays Hill there are many quiet and lovely ways by which to win back to Burley.

III

On our third venture we came down through Aldridge Hill to Boldresford Bridge, went through Waterford Copse, over the highway, and a few yards up the gravel road that passes behind the Balmer Lawn Hotel turned left into a gravel track. This track took us across Balmer Lawn, which is a big open space all gorse and grass with a pond and innumerable grazing ponies, and brought us through the gate into Pignalhill Enclosure, where are oaks, pines, birches, and a brick kiln. Soon after we had passed the kiln we turned left and came into the drive between Pignalhill and Pignal Enclosures, turned right and went through the first gate we came to on our right.

135

We were now in Perry Wood, with a long, straight, bumpy grass track in front of us, and round us acres of dry grass and pines of all ages and sizes poking up singly or standing in lines and bunches. It is not a very taking track, but it did its best to entertain us by sending little grey lizards rustling through the grass, a smutty coal-tit to do gymnastics in some baby pines, and hung two hawks in the air. When it drew near Woodfidley and the gravel road to Denny Lodge its borders blossomed with violets, restharrow, milkwort and dandelions.

All the same we welcomed the green shade of Woodfidley's oaks, pines, thorns, and hollies, though the new track was rock-like with hardened ruts and poachings. Bill hunted eagerly but found nothing, and this lack of game was explained to us by an elderly woodsman we met, who told us that the buckhounds had been here the day before and had killed not far from where we then were. He said the deer kept crossing the track quite close to him but did not heed him, being wholly occupied by the danger coming at them so noisily.

If I were rich as Croesus I would not hunt the deer, they are such timid things and have neither the black character of the fox nor anything like his chances of escape. And then their end is horrible, not swift like the fox's death, for I am told it means waiting, surrounded by the baying hounds, for a man with a rope and a knife.

For some queer reason hunted animals often turn to man when at the end of their resources, only to find he is more often than not without pity. A fox took shelter in an empty cradle and was thrown to the hounds because

136

he was given away by the baby's mother ; a deer tried to hide in a cottage porch and was driven away though utterly spent.

But there are people who are exceptions to the rule and of one of these I know. He is an oldish man, a small-holder, who did his best to save a hunted deer. The wretched beast had run through a gate on to his land in the last stages of terror and despair. 'Her was panting like a sheep, poor toad, and her legs were shaking under her, and the eyes of her starting out of her head.' He shut the gate, for he heard the hunt close at hand, and stood there to defy them. When they came they tried to chaff and cajole him into opening it, because, for some reason I forget, they could not get at the deer except by the gate. But he would not budge, nor was he silent. 'There's not a lady nor a gentleman among the lot on you,' he cried, ' chivying a poor animal so ! You'm on'y too ready to county court the likes of us for chaining of a dawg up, and you'd have plenty to say if I was to draive my horse when he were going a bit tender, or if a lad catched a bullock a clout or two. But 'taint no harm to draive and draive one of they poor deer till her's like to die ov fraight without you stick a knife in her throat. Oh my dear heart, no ! That's just a bit ov fun, that is ! '

My informant came home full of it but had to admit that the old man fought in vain, because by dint of screeches and cracking thongs the hunters terrified the deer into breaking out.

Though the rides running up to the beech-crowned

knoll, that is the glory of Woodfidley (and a valuable landmark to the wanderer on the southern moors), beckoned us shamelessly we kept on down our rough track till it brought us to a gate near a railway bridge and out on to Bishop's Dike. The line runs through Perry Wood and Woodfidley, and several hidden trains had rattled by whilst we were walking along, and now we saw the embankment driving right across the Dike and stayed to watch two trains charging towards each other like tilting knights. Their smoke went writhing and twisting over the heather, lingering till the trains had gone, and then thinned, broke up and vanished.

Bishop's Dike is about five hundred acres of bog and heather enclosed by a squat, wambling earthwork with a ditch on either side. In spite of its dangerously deep holes this bog, one of the worst in the Forest, is regularly grazed by ponies, whose instinct I suppose warns them when they are near a really bad place. The head keeper, who lives at Denny Lodge, a most charming person, told me that he had slipped into one of the holes and had sunk up to his armpits almost at once, adding that if it had happened at night he doubts whether he would have got out again.

The Dike, Ditch or Purlieu, as it is variously called, must have been much sounder in the day of John Pontoise, Winchester's bishop under Edward I, if the legend of how that prelate came to possess it is true. They say that the king told him he might have as much land in the Forest as he could crawl round in a day, and that the bishop devised himself a machine which would help him to cover

138

a considerable area and still keep within the terms of the agreement.

The machine consisted of two wheels with a sort of padded axle across which the bishop lay and propelled himself along at quite a respectable pace with his hands and feet.

It is delicious to think of the figure he must have presented bumping through the heather, struggling up the rises, free-wheeling down the slopes, and possibly coming a purler over a family of wild boars wallowing in the mud. But he was sure to have had a retinue of monks, squires, and men-at-arms to go ahead and scare away any lurking buck, boar, or wolf, to prod the ground where it looked unsafe for the passage of the episcopal machine, and to do a little judicious pushing and shoving when the going got too bad.

We turned left along a good sound track with Woodfidley and Denny Lodge on our near side and the bog on our right. The track went up a green mound where, under oaks and thorns, primroses and violets grew, and then, bearing away from the woods, shrank to a footpath and through pines and gorse took us down to Denny Bog.

Woodfidley is looked upon as a rain brewer in the Forest, a lengthy downpour from this quarter being called Woodfidley rain, and as we came through it the sky had become suitably overcast. Under the dark clouds Denny Bog looked beautiful and terrifying, a Red Indian of a bog with its dwarf forests of rufous sweet gale and coppery pools and waterways. A beechern crest, part of Denny

Wood, stood above it and the rising moors further helped to shut it in and keep it secret and hidden.

As we crossed it by means of its three flat bridges a mallard left a runnel, going away on whistling wings, and something heavy slabbered over the mud behind some rushes. Fortunately I was able to restrain Bill from plunging after the unseen beast and was glad to reach the sound track on the other side; it runs under great oaks, past the bungalows and fields of Denny Settlement and joins the gravel road to Denny Lodge.

The Lodge, a gabled red house, is built on the rise above the Settlement, and behind it we found a charming path which wound in and out among beautiful oaks, beeches, and young birches to Denny Enclosure.

By the gate is a pound, so that it is easy to recognise. Denny is a gorgeous assembly of oaks and beeches, hollies, thorns, and birches, growing closely enough to appeal to the wild things and yet allowing the sun plenty of rein. We followed the broad grass ride down a steep hill and up another, at the top of which another ride crossed ours. Here we turned left and at the end of the new track came out on the broad, heathy stretch dividing Denny and Parkhill Enclosure.

The first part of the way through Parkhill is lined by enormous conifers, and then come other trees, mostly oaks I think, thickly massed together and popular with deer, judging from the slot we saw. We found two other things besides the deer slot. In a hoof-print sat a glow-worm, or what I take to have been one, for when I turned her over with a grass blade I found she had three little phos-

phorescent bands under her tail. She looked very dashing
in her nigger-brown jacket edged with tiny bone-coloured
spots, and showed to great advantage against the pale clay
of the hoof-print. I have a quaint old book on insects,
written in the form of letters exchanged between two
girls called Felicia and Constance, and illustrated with
excellent line engravings. Felicia having found a glow-
worm writes of her discovery, and after explaining to her
friend that the light of the female is a ' dazzling invitation '
to the male says :

' Dr. Darwin alludes to this beautiful phenomenon in
the following lines, addressed to the Nymphs of Fire :

> " Warm on her couch, the radiant worm,
>   Guard from cold dews her love-illumin'd form :
>   From leaf to leaf conduct the virgin light,
>   Star of the earth, and diamond of the night ! " '

Having replaced the love-illumined worm on her several
feet we went on again, and soon after caught sight of a
plant I have always longed to find growing wild. It was
the flower called by some Joseph and Mary, and, by the
less poetic, lungwort.

It is not common, and I understand only grows wild in
Hampshire, Dorset and the Isle of Wight. It stood erect
and alone on a grass bank, a pretty thing, its narrow leaves
mottled with pale green, its buds and young flowers pink,
its older blossoms a deep and heavenly blue.

The Forest and Dorset share one or two exquisite things
besides lungwort, blue gentian among them. I have not
found gentian here yet, but there is a Dorset heath
where I have seen it flourishing on a rather boggy slope

amongst sparsely growing heather, and as I had ridden about this heath for months before finding the gentian colony I still have hopes of coming across some in the Forest. That Dorset heath is a blessed stretch of solitude and grows, as well as gentian, heather and gorse, a tiny golden-white wild rose bush which never seems to get higher than a foot from the ground and whose leaves smell of apples.

In Parkhill is the site of Lyndhurst Old Park, whose pannage as recorded in 1300 was worth 34s. 3d. ' when the acorn comes,' and its yearly yield of honey at 2s. The salt-way from Lymington to Southampton came through Parkhill, but I do not know whether it is still traceable.

Outside Parkhill Enclosure we crossed a tree-girdled, daisied green and entered Ramnor Enclosure by the gate near Ramnor Cottage. Here a gravel track, bearing right-handed past a group of young wild cherry trees in full blossom and with wild violets blooming at their feet, went down a steep hill from whose top we had a glorious view over the trees to the Brockenhurst Moors.

Trees cover the track all the way from Ramnor to the highway where it runs into Brockenhurst. On one side is Balmer Lawn, the scene of pony races in the past, and away on the other are the kennels of the buckhounds from whence sometimes come some grand samples of hound music.

We got back to Burley along the moor road to Vinney Ridge, leaving it at Clumber Enclosure for the track across Ober Water, through Ferney Knap to Markway Hill.

CHAPTER IX

BURLEY'S MOORLANDS

If the woods near Burley are beautiful so are the moors, and though they do not offer the same chances of seeing deer, fox, or badger, they afford some splendid walks.

Perhaps the best of these is the one we took across the moors lying on the northern boundary of Oakley and reaching as far as Bratley Wood. It was the first we discovered, and so there are two reasons for its taking pride of place in this chapter.

Early one April morning when the cherry and thorn blossom were at their best we set out for Burley Street, and on reaching it turned down a road close to the post-office. In this village the cottages have pretty gardens, the farms allow their pigs to slumber in the middle of the road, and cows and ponies graze perilously above car level on top of the roadside banks. There are two ways opposite the post office, one going to Burley Moor and the other to Vereley (pronounced Vurley), which is a collection of private houses and beech trees on the edge of Picket Plain.

The Burley Moor road runs under trees for about a quarter of a mile, passing through a stream flowing down from Backley Plain to Mill Lawn, and shortly after reaches Burley Moor. Here it turns sharply to the right as if shying away from the red house standing at the foot of the moor, and hurries off to join the Burley Lodge road. Two sandy tracks come down the moor and meet near the house ; it was the right-hand of these two that we followed.

As we climbed up to Berry Beeches, which is the wood

A Roadside Cottage

covering the ridge between Burley Moor and Backley Plain, the warm brown dome of Ridley Wood rose above Vereley's descending trees, and behind Ridley we recognised Picket Plain's spartan line; ahead the tawny vale called Harvest Slade Bottom slowly unfolded itself, and on the right, beyond the medley of house and tree that is Burley, there showed the crest of the moor above Mill Lawn.

The trees of Berry Beeches are old and have not tasted the bitterness of pollarding, but they are sufferers from ingrowth, which ' catches' them in the stem. Unlike most beech woods, where, as a rule, nearly all plant life is choked by the mass of mast and leaf shed by the trees, Berry encourages grass, bracken, bramble and moss to grow under its shelter with the most charming results.

It is said that vipers favour this ridge, but we have not come across one here. A viper's bite is very painful and makes the bitten member assume revolting proportions, but it is seldom that it proves fatal. One of the reasons for this is that the victim is usually bitten through clothing, such as a stocking or trouser-leg, which wipes off a good bit of the poison from the fangs before they pierce the flesh. Adders, or vipers, whichever you like to call them, are very timid like all wild things, and will not attack unless trodden upon or cornered by some nit-wit with a stick. If left alone they will be only too glad to whip away into hiding.

Should you be unfortunate enough to get bitten the best thing to do is to tie something tightly above the bite —that is, between the wound and the heart, make it bleed freely and rub permanganate of potash into the punctures if you happen to be among the wise few who carry some of these crystals in a pocket. Then get as quickly as possible to a doctor.

The Forest adders are variously coloured putty, reddish-brown, or silver-grey, but they all have the dark zig-zag pattern down their backs which is the unmistakable hall-mark of their kind. Besides adders there are in the Forest the harmless grass snake and smooth snake, the latter a rare creature said to be found only in the New Forest and the adjoining Dorset heaths.

Before the time of Mr. Bundy and Bill I had a black cross-bred dog called Smuggler, who was, contrary to the accepted theory regarding 'mongrels,' a delicate dog. In spite of his many physical drawbacks, which included an unnatural degree of rotundity, we all adored him on account of his angelic character. One day in Dorset he and I were walking on the cliffs near Swanage when a heavy, red adder crawled slowly across the path. Poor Smuggler, like Henry King, had a weakness for chewing little bits of string, and promptly fell upon the snake, whereupon he was bitten through the lip before he had time to rectify his error. Within ten minutes he became too ill to walk, and I had to labour home with him in my arms under a broiling sun. Swelling did not set in before we got back, but when it did he was a terrible sight. Both eyes disappeared, his neck became a rigid block, his tongue was paralysed. He could not lie down or lap the milk and brandy a wise old labourer, whose advice we had asked, had told us to give him, remarking of the brandy, ' it takes p'ison to kill p'ison.' The vet. who came at last looked coolly at the sufferer, said he would die, and left well satisfied with himself. A dismal family we sat up all night and kept ladling brandy and milk down Smug's throat and hoping for the best. By morning he could bend his neck and lap milk, by the evening was free from pain, and by the end of about ten days all trace of swelling had gone. The only lasting effect the bite had upon him was the patch of white hair which came where the fangs had entered.

I recount this tale of misadventure to comfort anyone whose dog may get bitten by a snake, for it shows that even an unhealthy subject can survive a nasty bite in a dangerous place. In Sewell's *Dog's Medical Dictionary* it says, 'Apply a ligature as tightly as possible above the part bitten and apply a saturated solution of permanganate of potash (Condy's fluid undiluted) to the wound. Give stimulants, as brandy or sal volatile, freely, the latter well diluted with water.'

We came out through hollies, a few last beeches and deep bracken on to Backley Plain. On either side of the worthy track, sound and gravelled and choosing the best parts of the moor for its journey to Bratley Woods, the moors roll away in deep troughs and swelling crests, stuck with bleached pines killed in youth by pitiless winds or by fires, and sprinkled with knots of sturdy hollies. From the high places we could see the Dorset and Wiltshire downs, and looked over shelving woods to the Isle of Wight and Sway's lofty tower, one of the many 'follies' to be found in the south-west of England. In the dips gravel banks got up and shut out the views ; gorse leant from the tops to dangle its spike-guarded gold nuggets over our heads ; and hollies crowded together in sufficient numbers to shelter several deer.

We passed the wood called Backley Beeches and just beyond it crossed another track in which ours came to an end ; here we took to a footpath running through the heather on the right of the new track. By then we were close to and facing Bratley Wood, but keeping to our path bore away from it to the right, passed through some young pines, and neighboured on the right by the sweetly named Stinking Edge Wood, descended to a stream. A bank carries the path down to the stream, a bridge hoists it over, and then it works its way up the opposite slope until it reaches the gravel track coming down from the Ringwood highway through Bratley Wood to Oakley. Higher up another track branches off from the Ringwood-Oakley one; it goes over Bratley Water, up the heathery side of Mogshade Hill and joins the Emery Down road near Boldrewood Green.

Turning up the hill we soon reached Bratley Wood, whose fine oaks and beeches are feeling the hand of time and stand about their dead or dying comrades solemnly surveying their ruin and appearing to meditate on the sad truth that all flesh is grass. Though of no great size and close to the noisy Ringwood road it is an impressive old wood and has the honour of entertaining a pair of buzzards.

The birds were aloft when we arrived at the wood, and for several minutes we stood watching their splendid

148

manœuvring. Martin Armstrong in his poem 'The Buzzards' has described their flight both accurately and beautifully. He says :

. . . Serenely far there swam in the sunny height
A buzzard and his mate who took their pleasure
Swirling and poising idly in golden light.
On great pied motionless moth-wings borne along,
  So effortless and so strong,
Cutting each other's paths, together they glided,
Then wheeled asunder till they soared divided
Two valley's width (as though it were delight
To part like this, being sure they could unite
So swiftly in their empty, free dominion),
Curved headlong downward, towered up the sunny steep,
Then, with a sudden lift of the one great pinion,
Swung proudly to a curve and from its height
Took half a mile of sunlight in one long sweep.

It is a pity that with such a noble appearance the bird should have a coward soul. But such, say the ornithologists, is the case. If a game bird be wounded and crouching in some covert then the buzzard will drop upon him ; if a baby-rabbit be out by itself, then the buzzard will attack ; but he will not tackle a hale and hearty grouse or a full-grown rabbit, will even fly before the onslaught of that dear bird the olive-coated, pig-tailed plover. A thrush will defend its nest with desperate valour against cat or man, a partridge will tumble about in the dust within a foot or two of a pursuing dog and his master, pretending a mortal hurt in order to distract the hunter's attention from her brood and give it time to escape. But not the buzzard ; he, as a rule, is content to circle about

149

his nest, watching its violation from a safe distance and making a whining complaint but offering no resistance to the rape of his eggs. Sometimes, however, when instead of eggs his fluffy white young are in the leaf-lined bundle of sticks which constitutes their home, he will come at unwelcome visitors in no uncertain manner, and then it is best to be off for his talons and beak are weapons worthy of a soldier and can deal nasty wounds.

We stayed until our buzzards left us, drifting away on some air current which carried them out of sight over Mogshade Hill, and then we turned our backs on Bratley Wood and keeping close to the highway made our way over the heather until we came to Handy Cross. Here we found the good gravel track which bearing left runs to a bush-filled dip, clambers out again, passes a clump of trees called Little Wood, and drives straight through the magnificent beeches of Ridley Wood.

In Queen Elizabeth's time a man called, I believe, John Marlowe was prosecuted for pollarding the trees. His ' crime ' served two good purposes. Firstly, that of giving us a good idea of the wood's age ; secondly, of lengthening the life of the trees, for it is held in many quarters that what monkey glands do for the aged human early pollarding does for timber. In this wood the operation has not had the effect of making the beeches short, top-heavy, and brawny, as it so often does, but has added to their beauty. From stately trunks flawless boughs shoot up straight and tall like the lances of an army of giants ; no ingrowth here, no horrid misshapen monstrosity. The trees do not crowd each other but grow close enough to hide the sky when all their leaves are out. Birds and squirrels love Ridley, and though the birds may become silent and the squirrels hide if a body of laughing and talking people march through the wood, if you come quietly they will not mind you much. Indeed, one squirrel exchanged long stares with us from the branch of a young tree off which we could have poked him with a coach whip if we had been low-minded enough to want to bring him down. We tried to make him curse us by 'chattering' at him, as we had been told it was quite easy to do, but his calm look of enquiry putting us to shame we apologised and left him.

Near the end of the wood our track is crossed by one coming down from Picket Plain and going up to Berry Beeches. It has a messy stretch near the stream in Harvest Slade Bottom and also clay pockets, into one of which sometime since poor Mr. Bundy fell and nearly got smothered before I missed him. It was much softer than ordinary clay pockets, about the consistency of cream, and the poor little dog was floundering blindly in it, his eyes and nose full of mud. When I got him out it took me a good ten minutes to remove the worst of the yellow slime with which he was coated. Bad pockets are marked by those who find them with tall saplings, so if you come across a slender rod sticking up in the middle of a path leave it alone as it is there for a very good reason.

As we did not want to return to Berry Wood we kept on with our track, following it out of the wood and down a boggy heathered slope, over a stream, up through Vereley's northern beeches, till it met with the gravel road which ends opposite Burley Street post office.

151

If we had not had to rejoin Miss Riley at the post office and were walking back to Ringwood we should have skirted the Vereley trees and kept to a track bearing right-handed up the heather, crossed the Burley road on top of Picket Plain and entered a footpath which soon drops down into Foulford Bottom, to scramble out of it at once and come to an end in a gravel road. We should have turned left down the road, gone past a charming white house with an orchard and come out on to the Hightown road. A little way down on the right, at the end of the common, there is a lane with a thick hedge on either side. It leads to a gravel lane which runs into another little road connecting the Ringwood highway with the High-town road. Almost opposite the meeting place of lane and little road, by the side of a small house, there is a stile and a footpath. Prosperous fowls inhabit the paddocks on one side of the path, and brown-and-white goats with shaggy plus fours those on the other side. Sometimes children are playing in the goats' paddock, so it is a pleasant path to walk along. Over the next stile there is an odd-shaped little field where an ancient pony is usually grazing, and over the third lies a big cultivated bit of land belonging to one of the jolliest farmers imaginable. He has curls all over his head, a bronzed face, little twinkling eyes, has travelled all over the world as a gunner, and possesses an enormous laugh. Fortunately, he does not mind people crossing his land if they keep to the foot-paths.

The last stile is close against the wall of his thatched farmhouse, and brings you out on to the Hightown road again. Bear right-handed, take the first turning on the left after passing the house called Old Stacks, and there lies before you the long stretch of tarmac and bungalows and villas that leads to Ringwood station past the cemetery and school.

II

Another moorland walk which we find entirely satisfying we took on a cloudless day in April.

We started off through the trees opposite Burley School and bearing left soon came up with a sandy path running across the top of Goatspen Plain. All round us the country, which Walter Scott loved because he said it reminded him of his native moors, lay in uneven folds reaching away to long hills crested with pines. It was not too hot on the plain, though the heat haze had blotted out the Dorset downs and set the horizon hills dancing and the sun had fired the windows of the houses on Thorney Hill, making them flash like diamonds among their trees. A light breeze was about its pleasing job of fanning the gorse blooms and mingling their golden smell with the good summer scent drawn out by the sun from the lilac sand under our feet.

We went briskly over the plain and down into the green-brown bottom called Holmsley Bog, where the path steps over two waterways belonging to Avon Water and crosses the railway line running through the bottom by means of red brick Greenberry Bridge. On the other side of the bridge we passed a clump of pines and hollies, and when we gained the top of the hill saw the dark pine tree frame of

153

Holmsley Enclosure and the range of white buildings that is Holmsley Lodge.

Here we joined the gravel road which runs from Durmast and the Closes across Goatspen Plain through Holmsley to the Lyndhurst highway.

Holmsley Enclosure, planted in 1811 and spoken of by Wise as a young plantation, is now in parts a dense wood of oaks and Scots pines which grow over a rare tangle of hollies, brambles, bracken, and lichened thorns. Birds love it and were loud in its praise that day, but so thick was the mesh of twig and leaf above and the bushes below that we never caught a glimpse of the singers. A few primroses grow on the banks of the fences, where after one look at the jungle under the trees they seem to have very wisely decided to remain, for no flower could survive in those choked fastnesses which seem to be designed only for the safe conduct of foxes coming here with hounds hot on their heels.

It was in Holmsley and about this time of the year that I witnessed a wonderful act of valour, the hero of which was a fox. He was in bad case, having gone to earth within easy reach of the means for digging him out. The field was mostly sitting on the roadside banks, their reins over the heads of their grazing mounts, fanning themselves with bracken to keep off the flies. The lad with the spade had got within sight of the poor fellow and had turned for instructions to the master when with glorious courage the fox leapt out into the air, flung himself backwards over the top of the ruined earth within a few yards of the assembled pack, and sped off into the friendly bushes.

154

What a scramble there was when we heard the horn sounding ' Gone away ' instead of the fox's dirge ! At the first note of the scandalised hounds the horses were fighting to be off, and their riders struggling to get the reins back over their heads and fling themselves into the saddle all at the same time. I am glad to say that Dan Russell, having cast the enclosure behind him, raced across the moors and went securely to ground again in a nice stony bit where he was left to rest on his laurels.

Something under half a mile from the Lodge we came to where side by side two streams flow out of the wood, titter down little falls, cross the road and disappear between primrose banks into the trees again. Above them on the right we saw a gate opening on to the ride we wanted, which runs westward through the enclosure to Thorney Hill.

We found this part of the enclosure very different from that which had been on the Burley side of the streams, for instead of oaks and undergrowth massed together our way lay through wide clearings deep in bleached grasses and thinly scattered with pines. It was very hot in the enclosure as there was no shade, and what trees there were kept the breeze away. The birds were represented by a single chiff-chaff, and the only other signs of life were a lot of brown speckled butterflies which were hovering like little dusty leaves above the dry grasses.

For some time the track went straight, then bore right, crossed a stream, went up a gravelly, heather-tufted hillock and bearing left ran for a while under trees. It was not a comfortable track to walk on, for it was badly poached by horses and had deep ruts, all of which holes and corrugations the sun had baked as hard as iron. On the other hand, when we got to the stream, and later to the shady bit above the hillock, we found it still spongy after a fortnight's drought. Having left the trees and gained another clearing it mended its ways, like a sort of death-bed repentance, and for the few remaining yards between us and the gate became a thoroughly respectable gravel footway.

Before leaving the enclosure we stopped to look at a huge ants' nest on the side of the track. The creatures themselves, great copper-coloured horrors, were swarming over it in such numbers that there arose from the heap a noise like a simmering kettle, or light rain on dry leaves. They made Mr. Bundy quite nervous, and even Bill refrained from investigating the moving mound, standing at a respectful distance with wrinkled forehead, ears cocked and a puzzled expression in his eyes.

Outside the gate we lay down under some splendid pines to cool off and share biscuits, looking at the billowy moors and droves of holly bushes before us, and listening to the murmur of traffic on the Lyndhurst highway, the hushing of the wind in the dark boughs above us, and the muffled thunder of the guns on Salisbury Plain. The breeze brought us the fitful clonking of cowbells, and once the hoarse cuck-cuck of a cock pheasant, the faint smell of wood fires, and now and then the barking of a dog.

When we got up, and I had brushed the pine-needles off myself and Mr. Bundy (they do not stick to Bill's slippery coat), we set off down the right-hand fork of the track

156

ahead and were soon among the hollies. For some while we had seen the smoke of fires belonging to the gypsy encampment on Thorney Hill, and soon we came in among bushes hung with their unlovely rags. Grubby heads poked over the gorse to stare at us, and hoarse whisperings of ' 'Oo's she ? ' and ' What she want here, I ask ? ' came to our ears.

We didn't enjoy that part of the walk very much, and I hurried ashamedly when a poor idiot wobbled to his feet from beside a grey tent, let out a goblin yell and gesticulated wildly to us. He meant no harm, in fact I think he was being hospitable, but his kindly intentions only made us more desirous of getting through the holms and on to the moors again.

We caught up with a motherly old gypsy woman who, dressed in many colours, was carrying a bag of wood on her back with the ease of a youth. I asked her if the scattered yews and hollies through which we had come and among which we were still walking were really Thorney Hill Holms, as I had been led to expect a holly wood of considerable denseness. She told me that these were the Thorny Hills Holms, lady, but that fire had burned away a-many of the trees and was a cruel thing to hollies and did more harm to them than rabbits. Rabbits I gathered gnaw the bark off in rings, and then the tree gives up the ghost. She was a dear old thing and obligingly directed us to a sandy path on the right which took us out of the trees and on to the heather above Whitten Bottom.

It was lovely there on the hill. Whitten Pond lay like

157

an acquamarine in a pale jade ring amongst the sombre heather away down in the bottom—a brilliant accent in a landscape of heathy ridges and valleys, and low, wooded hills. On our left the tarmac road ran down from Thorney Hill to Burley Beacon, to our right a broken patch nicking the top of the nearest rise of the moor showed us where the track we wanted lay.

A jolly boy in a brown sweater galloped by us on a stout bob-tailed pony, scattering the yellow cows lounging in the track and disappeared over the ridge. We watched the pair bobbing up the opposite slope and then set off soberly in their wake down the hill and into the dip, where we found we had to traverse a boggy bit with a wriggling gutter in it. Having managed it successfully we gained the top of the slope, and here we met the breeze again and had delicious country to look at. Another horseman, a young farmer on a pulling black pony colt, bore down upon us so furiously that we had to leap out of the track into the heather, much to the dismay of a hen pheasant who rose like a bombshell from under our feet and frightened us out of our wits.

The path brought us back to Holmsley Lodge, and, as we did not want to go back to Burley by the same way as we had left it, we turned left down a grass path when we got to Greenberry Bridge and walked beside the railway line to the level crossing opposite Shappen Bottom.

The short journey was enriched by the arrival of two wheatears who accompanied us as far as the crossing, flitting ahead and perching on the wires of the fence or the telegraph wires to wait for us to catch up. They were

158

quite bewitching, with their pearly-hued bodies, dark flight and tail feathers, broad white tail band, and fetching black masks. They seemed very glad to see us, for they kept bowing delightedly and encouraging us to follow with jovial chack-chackings.

Their predilection for wire as a perch reminded me of a wonderful experience in my childhood. It was in Cornwall, and I was out on the cliffs with an aunt who had consented, with all appearance of willingness, to climb to the edge of the railway cutting near Hawk's Point and wait for the train to go by from St. Ives. While we waited a cuckoo flew up from some gorse bushes, pitched on the wire fence of the cutting, and started to cuckoo. At such close quarters its voice sounded strange, much deeper, a trifle hoarse, and oddly human. We stood spellbound, and I was delighted to see that the bird tilted forward as it called, just like the cuckoo in our nursery clock.

The wheatears forsook us at the crossing, perhaps on account of the cottage there, so we continued up Shappen Bottom without them. The bottom is a narrow fold in the moors with a line of alders growing on the edge of a bog where sweet gale also blows and where foxes like to lurk.

A springy path, the work of the turfing iron, runs along the bottom till it comes to a green with a pretty cream-washed cottage backed by little hills covered in hollies, oaks, and beeches. Fat fowls stroll over the green where once the May Day dances were held, apparently untroubled by the proximity of the fox-sheltering willows in the nearby bog. No doubt the varmint takes his toll of

159

the poor addle-pates, for nothing is more obstinately idiotic than a fowl. We were told of one Forest farmer whose poultry refuse to shelter in the safe houses he provides for them and prefer to roost in the trees from whose boughs they can easily be wheedled by the average fox. To scare the fox away the farmer has perforce to hang the trees with lamps, which must make the little holding look very charming when the moon is up.

Behind the cottage is the gravel road which joins the Burley road opposite the school.

CHAPTER X

IN THE
HUDSON COUNTRY

L

O<small>NE</small> day I was reading Elizabeth Godfrey's book on the New Forest and discovered there what I had always longed to know, the identity of W. H. Hudson's ' House on the Boldre.' It was in this house that he began and ended *Hampshire Days*, the guest of a family after his own heart, people who kept neither cat nor dog, and who in their relations with the wild things practised his creed of ' pet nothing, persecute nothing.'

On learning the whereabouts of the house I felt like a certain great man who loved the works of Isaac Walton, and discovered in one of them a confession that the old angler had carved his initials on a pillar in (I think) Westminster Abbey. Seizing candle and matches, for it was evening, the devotee dashed hatless and in slippers across the way and searched the abbey until he found the precious letters.

As I could not set out at once, for it was late and Brockenhurst is some miles from Ringwood, I did the next best thing, which was to map out a route pleasing to myself and to the dogs and arrange for a very early start next morning.

The spring day broke cloudless and warm so we drove to Burley, and leaving Miss Riley in the heather of Clay Hill went along the track running up and down across a corner of the moor, dashed across the Lyndhurst highway when the traffic gave us the chance and entered Wilverley Enclosure.

Wilverley is full of hills and dells, is partly filled with pines but has a good percentage of oaks and beeches to make up for them, and is often visited by deer.

162

On entering it we took the right-hand of the two tracks meeting at the gate. At first we found it disappointing, for our way ran flatly between adolescent and infant pines protected by wire-netting fences, but soon the netting stopped, the trees got bigger and the air became charged with the subtle, dusty, resinous smell breathed out by adult conifers. Then the track dropped steeply, on the right the pines gave way to sunny oakwoods, and in front we looked across a green valley and mounting oaken crests to a hill topped by a handsome knot of firs. From the greenwood came the song of birds, the laugh of woodpeckers and the grasshoppery noise of a chiff-chaff among them ; but from the young pines on the left there was no sound. These little trees, planted close together in straight lines, shed such a blackness that it was almost like looking from night to day to turn from their cold, murky ranks to the bright oakwoods opposite.

At the bottom of the dell we took a grass ride on our left. It was lined with pines, but we passed a fine wayside beech and caught glimpses through fuscous trunks of other silver boles rising out of a ruddy mound, before the pine branches closed completely over the path and turned it into a gloomy tunnel.

Here Bill got wind of some deer and disappeared for some minutes, anxious ones for me because he had gone away in the direction of the Lymington highway where a buckhound had been killed not long before. The poor thing had plunged out of the enclosure and on to the tarmac just in time to connect with a passing car.

At the top of the track, which in rising sharply had lost

163

its coniferous canopy, I sat down with Mr. Bundy under a group of big fir trees, straining my ears for news of Bill's return and indulging in bouts of whistling and calling. At last he reappeared, a killer to all appearances, for his mouth was red with the blood from his tongue, which being long lolls out and gets torn on the thorns and brambles he crashes through in his haste.

Above the firs we came to a medley of tracks, bore right, then left, and then went ahead past a nursery of bright green young larches where Bill found more deer only to lose them at once. I heard the noise of their going and saw the swaying green trail they left but never caught a glimpse of them.

Almost at once we came to the south-eastern border of Wilverley, and over the gate looked across a brief bit of moor and the oaks of Setthorns to Sway's lofty tower and the Island's downs.

Making for Setthorns we got down to the gravel road which comes from the Lymington highway, crosses the Avon Water valley, and eventually by devious ways arrives at the coast. We went up it for a few yards on our left till we found the narrow sandy path running between the heathery crests of Yew Tree Bottom, under the railway bridge, to Setthorns.

One side of this little valley had been fired, purposely I think, because the other side was untouched and the blackened grass ended neatly at the path's edge. This firing is done to rid the slope of gorse and heather and so give the ground a chance to grow feed for the ponies. The charred furze is used for fuel and burns well in any grate.

It was not easy to reach the other side of the bridge for the land was waterlogged, a contretemps not the least disconcerting to Bill but harassing to Mr. Bundy and myself.

Having got through the arch, in whose crannies were primroses by the dozen, we found ourselves confronted by the bog through which Avon Water flows and where insect hunters are said to be in the seventh heaven. To us it looked scrubby, dull and singularly uninviting, but though Setthorns lay close on our left we wandered a little way down its track to give it the chance of revealing some hidden beauty. We found nothing to detain us and retraced our steps, more hurriedly than we should have done on account of a smart pony stallion who showed unmistakably that he resented our presence near his quite unattractive harem.

A sulching passage with quavering hags for stepping-stones brought us back into the path to Setthorns. It runs rather unnoticeably off to the left on leaving the arch, tops a hillock, and so goes into the wood.

Setthorns is all ups and downs—grass, bracken, wild-flowers, slender oaks, sunny clearings, and plentiful thorny, tangled shelter for small beast and birds. At the top of the wood is a spacious tableland with a scattering of trees through whose trunks we saw first the woods and moors of Rhinefield Walk and later Sway's tower and the Island.

I believe I am right in saying that the tower was built by a Mr. Petersen, who intended it for his mausoleum and set a light on its top when it was finished. The result of this uncharted beacon was such confusion in the Sólent traffic that the Admiralty sent people to investigate and poor Mr. Petersen was made to dowse his glim.

Some while ago I went to visit the tower because I had been told that the views from the top were magnificent, but after an involved journey down tortuous lanes I arrived to find the tower a gaunt shell with broken windows and locked door.

A leftward bearing from the gate of Setthorns brought us on to the road running from Wilverly to Lymington. We had not realised until now how hot the day had become, but the two-miles-long stretch of unshadowed tarmac cutting straight ahead through the plain made it almost brutally clear. At first the road kept along the last reach above Longslade Bottom, then dropped into Whidden Bottom, where plovers and rooks were wheeling and disputing noisily, tunnelled under the railway whose banks were covered with primroses and windflowers, and then went up a back-breaking slope on to Setley Plain, where the gorse bushes came to its edge and made its last lap a golden alleyway. At the end of the alley we came out into the highway connecting Brockenhurst with Boldre and Lymington.

Boldre is a scattered village spread out along the valley of the stream whose name it bears. It has a charming old church standing some way off on a wooded hill, and therein hangs the great fourteen-holed bassoon with which the choir was led in Boldre's pre-organ days. The instrument was bequeathed to the church by a Mr. Jenvey whose descendants live in the village and still carry on as wheelwrights in their little old house near the river bridge.

166

William Gilpin, naturalist and author, was vicar of Boldre from 1771 to 1804. His tomb is behind the church in the north part of the graveyard where the poor of the parish were mostly buried. It was because of this the old man chose to be buried there, too. At least, so I have been told. Not long since I heard of a horrid superstition concerning the northern part of God's Acre. My informant said that in the old days the font was almost invariably placed between the north and south doors of a church, and during baptisms the north door was left wide open for the escape of the exorcised demons. These evil spirits, having left the church, encamped among the graves and took possession of the north part of the graveyard, thus making it highly unpopular as a burying-place. Naturally all those able to buy their few feet of ground never chose to lie north of the church, and so only paupers and penniless folk were put there.

Gilpin lived at Vicar's Hill. His house is a charming old building with a garden where many of the trees and plants he loved and cultivated are growing yet.

Between Lymington and Boldre are two earthworks of considerable age and some interest. Ampress, the smaller of the two, Mr. Sumner considers to have been a Jutish, Saxon or Danish seafarers' camp. Buckland Rings is the name of the big one towering above the main road ; it is tree-grown and commands noble views of the Island. Below it is Passford Farm, a delightful timbered cottage where food and drink is to be had, and above it is a fairly large house standing close to the road and nearly hidden by a high garden wall. In this house Southey lived after

167

his marriage with Catherine Bowles, the authoress of ' a series of ballads, domestic tales, and lyrics, which are marked by genuine pathos and simplicity of thought, with an unusual grace and harmony of versification.' Southey could be seen from the road hard at work near the window of one of the upper rooms, a small panelled apartment scarcely big enough for a really comfortable study.

We should not like to say whether Southey's house is in Boldre or Lymington, as it lies at the end of one and the beginning of the other. Near it is a small, beautiful old house, then comes a street of rather dull villas, and at the end of them is old Lymington. The town is quite charming and full of eighteenth-century houses, steep streets, shipbuilding yards, tiny quays and odd nooks and corners. It stands above the river and a great sweep of salt marshes with a sea-wall path running over them all the way from the town to Keyhaven. For some way the sea-wall keeps alongside the river, which is always fascinating, whether the tide is making and only the tops of the booms and reed beds show, or at ebb, when the lilac mudflats, smooth as silk, are exposed. The mudflats look so hard that the inexperienced might be tempted to get down on to them with the idea of exploring the tiny creeks and runnels of the reed beds, but disaster swift and smelly follows if you try. Bill once jumped on to them from the sea-wall and sank up to his neck ; it was a painful business rescuing him, and when I did get him out he was covered in blue-black slime and the odours arising from him were unspeakable.

From Keyhaven one can walk along a shingle bank to

Hurst Castle from whence the unhappy Charles the First made his last journey to London.

Fond as we were of both Boldre and Lymington we could not turn aside for them with Hudson's house for our goal. When we reached the highway we took the first left-hand turning we came to a little way down in the direction of Lymington. This was a narrow lane winding along between hedges and grass banks covered with wildflowers, downhill over a stream, and up again past cottages with pretty gardens, and dogs who rattle their chains and threaten furiously from the top of kennels roofed with vivid linoleum.

At the top of the hill we turned right, skirted a strip of uninteresting heath, and where the lane forked under a clump of pines went left and came out on to a tarmac road. This we followed downhill towards the wooded rise on which is Boldre church, and at the cross-roads near the river turned left.

By now I was all excitement for I knew that the trees ahead were those of Roydon Wood and so only half a mile lay between us and the 'House on the Boldre.'

We passed a few cottages and fields, and then a gate let us in among the grand old oaks and the wilderness of green bushes leading to Roydon Farm. The road runs up through the woods and joins the Lymington-Brockenhurst highway, so unless you take the right-hand turning when you reach the fork you will miss the sunburnt seventeenth-century house with its steep-pitched roof, tall chimneys, and creeper-covered walls which is Roydon Farm, the house by the Boldre.

I stood on the primrose-covered green in front of the house and gazed at the baby yew avenue in which Hudson found the nests of such fairy birds as gold-crests and long-tailed tits, and the outbuildings in which he discovered the retreats of other shy and tiny wildlings. It was here that he was able to watch the doings of a young cuckoo in a robin's nest, and so learned much about the innocent usurper's habits. It was here also that he witnessed the diverting affair between the hornet and the bank vole and the trickle of sap ; and in these woods it was that he saw the great spotted woodpecker clinging motionless to a sunlit tree, all black, white, and crimson, ' like a bird-figure carved from some beautiful vari-coloured stone.'

After a brief visit to the Boldre, flowing swiftly and shallowly past, I tore myself away from the house from which I felt that at any moment a tall, dark-bearded figure might suddenly emerge, and followed the dogs who were impatient to be up and away.

We rejoined the track, which climbed uphill under oaks and then at the top ran through some fine firs, and came out on to the highway between a little farm and fields full of wild daffodils.

Cutting across a bit of heath we got on to the road to Brockenhurst links and followed it downhill to where several roads and railway embankments met. Here we went left-handed under one arch and right-handed under another into a gravel track running uphill over moorland to a level crossing. A pretty, bashful girl was taking some time over opening the crossing gates for a young groom on a pony when we arrived, so we hurried tactfully over the rails and found ourselves first of all among some knolls crowned with beeches and hollies and then on a gorse-gilded heath.

Soon after passing a pine plantation, in the shade of which we saw an unromantic gipsy encampment, the track brought us face to face with the wooded hill called Hinchelsea and to the edge of Hinchelsea Bog. The famous bog lay between us and the wood, a wide expanse of cream-coloured reeds and red sweetgale, winding down a heathered valley and threaded by a stream whose clear waters were marred by discarded bric-a-brac from the gypsy camp.

The track is carried over the bog by low bridges and on the other side enters Hinchelsea almost at once. Hinchelsea is very old, its trees grow haphazard but close, they are of all kinds and are sturdy and fine. Some are swathed in moss, on others the ivy climbs to the top-most twigs, some grow waffle-like fungus, but we saw none diseased or distorted.

About midway through the wood we came upon a house, and turning away to the left followed a path that ran past a long, dark pool, so hidden from the sky by the trees that its water only mirrors their beauty and its own mossy banks.

Twisting in and out the path took us through a host of quaintly grown hollies and then on to Hinchelsea moor, where it turned sandy and thrust its way stubbornly through the heather to the edge of the Brockenhurst road.

By now we were all three so hot that instead of going straight ahead over Wilverley Plain we took to the tarmac and kept along by Wilverley Enclosure because the trees had flung their shadows across the road.

'The Naked Man,' a blanched and ragged little tree-wreck, is on Wilverley Plain. It is doubtful how many more winters he will stand for he looks in sad case, but when he falls there will be mourning in the Forest, for he is known all over it as a meeting-place and landmark.

II

Quite soon we went to Roydon Farm again, this time by car. The kind lady of the house allowed me to leave Miss Riley in the yard, introduced me to her black and white pink-footed pigeons, and before allowing me to depart showed me the inside of the house. Mr. Bundy and Bill had had to stop outside because Major, the brindled house-dog, objected to strangers of his species making free with his garden, and by the time I rejoined them I had learned that Roydon manor was granted to Netley Abbey by Henry the Third, that the date 1622 was carved on a stone inside the house, that the foundations were of stone and infinitely older than the rest of the building, and that the keeper would be greatly obliged if I kept the dogs on the lead until we were out of the woods because game was preserved in them.

We went down to the Boldre and found there a thorn tree in full blossom and a high timber bridge of greater solidity than is usually the case with New Forest bridges. This is because the stream, now hardly of sufficient depth to cover its bright green bunches of waterweeds, becomes in winter a ' broad, rushing, noisy river.'

Beyond the bridge the track mounted up between oak-woods where bluebells of a rare depth of colour flourished in thousands and rabbits abounded. Because of the rabbits our ascent was rapid and erratic, and I was thankful when the wood ended and a gate let us into a deserted lane, for I was beginning to wonder if it was possible to stand many more of Bill's terrific plunges as one tantalising creature after another hopped lazily across our path.

The lane's banks had hedges on top and were blue, white, and gold with wildflowers and rich in ferns. On either hand lay open fields, and at the end was Dilton Farm, a nice little place on top of a hill, with elm trees and barns and numerous large poultry houses. In the poultry pens were any amount of young ducks at the flapper stage, charming snowy things with smiling faces who ran about in companies whistling mellifluously, as yet of slender build and upright carriage and not fat, pouchy and waddling.

From the yard we descended to the foot of another hill up which we went past a pond nearly hidden by alders and a leaning oak, and on top walked across a rabbit-infested rough bit of ground where we saw two black sheep and a sooty lamb.

At the end of this field was a gate, and beyond the gate the free heath above Dilton. I unleashed the dogs and turned into a track on the left which took us downhill and past the few cottages of Dilton. All except one of these have mud walls and thatched roofs, each has a garden and a field or two lying between them and the woods behind. In front is a closely grazed space from which the gorse has been driven back, and only thorns and crab apples stand ; here the livestock of the hamlet pick a living. Ponies with tiny foals were either dozing in the sun as we came down or gazing across cottage gates at their fond owners, who seemed to want nothing better than to return stare for stare. From under the crooked trees came the clonking of the bells hung on broad straps about the necks of the gawky cattle lying in the shade, flapping their ears noisily, blowing, and chewing like Americans.

It always surprises me, knowing the impudent daring of foxes, that fowls should stray so far from safety to scratch, take dust-baths, and chase flies as near to the varmint's haunts as they possibly can. The well-to-do hens of Dilton are no exception, and I was watching one group on the fringe of the woods when I noticed among them a green woodpecker. A boy came from one of the cottages carrying a bowl of grain for the birds, so I asked him if the woodpecker was a tame one it seemed so at home and without fear. But he said ' no,' and that it would fly into a tree when he reached the fowls and would wait until he had gone before it came to earth again. This certainly happened, but it waited until he was quite close before it flew into the lowest branch of the tree above him, and left its perch again almost before he had turned his back.

The woodpecker was far tamer than the two little children we came across playing by the stream at the bottom of the hill. When they saw us coming they rose unsteadily to their feet and uttering frantic yells ran off as fast as their short legs could carry them. Thinking they were

174

scared of Bill I called him to heel and apologised to their mother, who, alarmed by their cries, had come running from her cottage. She said it was I, not the dog, of whom they were frightened, because no one came this way much and they had not seen a stranger before !

The brook where the children had been playing flows over the track, which then enters upon a lovely green stretch scattered with various breeds of tree, all gracefully grown and charming. Oak and beech, crab-apple and thorn, ash and holly are here on ground changing from turf to bracken, from bracken to heather, every few yards or so. We saw several jays, a magpie and many pheasants, and as we neared the Beaulieu road came upon two young men busy over the wood fire whose good smell and blue smoke had been drifting down to us and adding so much to the deliciousness of the morning air. Their small car, almost hidden by bracken, was sharing with the neighbour-ing enclosure fence the task of supporting the tarpaulin slung over their beds. The youths looked so pleased with everything they almost converted me to the idea of camp-ing, a business of which the thought alone—no bath and flies in the butter—usually fills me with cowardly dread.

About half a mile up the steeply rising Beaulieu highway we left the tarmac for the gravel track into New Copse Enclosure where oaks grow young and tall above some soft kind of grass, bracken and foxgloves. The way, level at first, soon begins to fall, crosses a clearing, and if fol-lowed to the end goes over a railway bridge into Perry Wood Enclosure. On one side of the bridge is a cottage where a keeper lives with some engaging fawn greyhounds ; on the other is a ride where lungwort grows.

We did not get as far as the bridge, but when we came to the clearing turned into a ride on our right. A group of young acacias stands at the beginning of this enchanting path where one wanders along stooping under low branches, through sunny clearings, finding all kinds of wildflowers and listening to the spring songs of the birds made bold by love and the secrecy of these unfrequented glades. Hosts of little bronze and brown butterflies haunt the grassy ruts, and in the clay are imprinted the feet of whole families of deer—the big slot of the buck, the smaller slot of the doe, and the minute prickings of the fawn.

We saw no deer, but in the rough grass on the edge of a clearing Bill found a family of pheasants. The mother-bird, squawking loudly, flew ignominiously away on squeaking wings, leaving her poults to save themselves as best they might. It was wonderful to see how quickly they disappeared, all save one on which Bill had instantly placed a paw with the deftness of a thief covering a dropped coin with his foot. He did not hurt the little thing and came away directly I called him, but the chick sat quite still, its darkly-striped body pressed tightly to the ground, its long neck stretched straight out and its funny little head cocked enquiringly on one side.

At the end of the ride we came upon the gravel road to Lady Cross Lodge, and crossed over it into one of the grassy tree-shaded rides of Frame Heath Enclosure. It was plentifully poached by deer, but we never saw a sign of them though we followed it for nearly three-quarters

A BIG OAK IN QUEEN BOWER

of a mile before turning up another ride on the right. This path took us out of the enclosure and into Frame Wood's oaks and pines, down the steep slope of Moon Hill and out into the green, gorsey bottom below Furzy Lodge.

On top of Furzy Lodge's hill are oaks, grass, and a row of cottages. When we arrived we found everybody busy washing clothes, hauling water from wells by means of long and curious sticks, tending timber waggons drawn by pony teams, or digging in gardens. We were greeted kindly by everyone except the dogs and one old rooster, who not only looked at us with hostility but made a few threatening steps towards us, coming broadside on and hooking his spur in his drooped wing.

I am not ashamed to admit to a hurried departure, for I have reason to know what a nasty customer such a bird can be. When I was a child we had a Wyandotte rooster who was a perfect tyrant. He conquered all his rivals in the farmyard and attacked the farmhands without fear, because, being protected by their leggings, they only laughed at him and never gave him the trouncing he deserved. Having seen him rout our stern old nurse and rip her apron down with his spurs we were terrified of him and never went near the yard until we had discovered his whereabouts. But one day in his pride and vainglory he went too far. The only male bird he had not crossed swords with was the turkey cock, a peaceful giant of great age and weight. Often the rooster had cast truculent glances at his rival and at last attacked the turkey furiously and without warning. The indignant old bird fell upon him, bore him to the ground, and sitting firmly down upon him waited until he had suffocated the rooster before he rose to his feet again.

A farmer told me he had just such another troublesome bird which saved itself from the pot in quaint fashion. This bird always attacked from behind, and it was this dastardly trick which laid him low in the end. The farmer's wife had hauled a bucket up to the top of the well and was leaning over to take it off the chain when she felt something strike her and slide scratching and fluttering over her head. Starting up she was just in time to catch a last glimpse of the feathered bully as he disappeared down the well.

The same man had a bantam cock under whose glittering breast-feathers beat the heart of a lion. " Praaper little soldier he were, forever vighten somethen', and though he got knocked about chronic he'd never quit till t'other was beat. It would have broke his heart to have met his master." So fond was the farmer of Banty that when he purchased a big black Indian gamecock, armed with formidable spurs, rather than allow the little creature to come against so terrible an adversary he took his new purchase down to a field some way from the farmhouse and there turned him loose with some pullets. But Banty heard the clear challenging crow and set off down the lane to find its owner. The farmer saw him go, but as he and all hands were busy with the hay he could not spare the time to try and save Banty from his fate.

It was late at night when they carried in the last load, and tired as he was the farmer was about to go down to

the gamebird's field to look for the body of his favourite
and give it honourable burial when a shout from one of
his men made him stop short. Coming up the moonlit
lane, staggering drunkenly from side to side, he saw a
bedraggled little object. It was Banty. He had lost an
eye, his comb and wattles were in tatters, he was caked in
dust and blood, but in his remaining eye shone a light
which truly said that the gamecock was dead.

Furzy Lodge is on the edge of Beaulieu Plain, Hudson's
'dreary waste,' and is linked with the Beaulieu highway
by a gravel road. This we followed and came on to the
tarmac near the large, irregularly shaped sheet of water
called Hatchet Pond. The pond gets its name from the
hatch gate a little farther along the road and was formed
by water filling up some old marl pits.

From the pond we walked over the heath to Stockley
Enclosure a mile and a half away. Keeping along its
border until we came to Pound Heath—the common above
Dilton—we followed a track which led us past a very big
barrow, and so came again to the gateway of Dilton Farm's
last field.

CHAPTER XI

BEAULIEU, BUCKLER'S
HARD, AND THE SALT-
MARSHES

I<small>F</small> it were not for the fact that game is preserved in all the coverts within easy reach of it, and if we had lost all hope of going back to the Isle of Purbeck, we should be content to live at Buckler's Hard. But it would be more than any of us could bear to have to walk through acres of enchanting woods and never stray from the public foot-path.

For a short stay of three, four, or perhaps five days and as a base for operations in the south, even though there is much road walking to be done before the free woods are reached, it is very good.

Two rows of cottages mellowed to that kindly hue which comes to Georgian brick after long acquaintance with mankind, run down to the Beaulieu river on either side of a wide street half grass, half gravel. At the end of one row is an engaging old building with small dormers, big windows, a charming doorway, and a sheet-metal vessel in full sail hung out from its wall as a sign. It is called The Master Builder's House and was the home of Henry Adams who constructed ships here, to the building of which went sometimes as many as two thousand oak trees.

' Agamemnon,' Nelson's ship in the Baltic, ' Swiftsure,' and ' Euryalus ' who played their part in Trafalgar Bay and several other big sixty-four and seventy-four gun vessels first tasted salt water from the slips of Buckler's Hard and, under shining new canvas, went their stately way to the sea between the oak woods that had given them birth.

182

THE CHAPEL AT BUCKLER'S HARD

It is recorded that when a launching was imminent it was not uncommon to have a crowd of ten thousand spectators, that stands were erected for their accommodation, and that every lane and byway was stiff with traffic—coaches, gigs, saddle-nags, ' pony-shays,' tumbrils, and tilt-waggons all bound for the Hard. The more important guests were entertained at the Master Builder's House, and on one occasion at least, I am told, royalty has sat under Henry Adams' roof.

All was happy and flourishing whilst the old man's hands held the wheel, but when death had folded them and his two sons took charge, disaster followed, though not at once. Flushed with success these unfortunates contracted to supply four men-o'-war to be delivered at one and the same time. It was too big an undertaking and they failed, were fined, went to law about the matter, and so brought ruin to themselves and their workpeople. One by one the houses disappeared, the yards fell into decay, and now only the two rows of cottages, the house, and a few seaweed-hung piles at the water's edge are all that is left of the village and slips which sent so many worthy ships to sea.

One of the cottages has been made into a delightful chapel. The walls are panelled with aged oak, the seats are plain and dark, the colour scheme blue, silver, and brown. In one corner is a fine old wooden statue of the Madonna, and the altar is hung with a piece of embroidered silk from Spain. The workmanship of this frontal is exquisite. On a blue ground little Chinese figures in gay garments attitudinize among tulips, roses, and carnations far bigger than they. A pink bird drinks from a pool with a fountain and a tree, and bunches of golden and white blossoms are scattered freely.

Bill was looking so dismally through the door whilst Mr. Bundy and I were admiring the chapel that we came out before I wanted to. I thought, also, that perhaps Mr. Bundy's presence, though he was tucked under my arm, might offend. Every vicar is not so Franciscan as one we met not long ago. He invited us all in, and when I demurred about the dogs, exclaimed, ' You surely don't imagine that anything man can build is too good to receive something made by God ? ' But the majority of folk quail at the idea of dogs entering churches and in the old days some parishes paid a person called a Dog Whipper to tan them out should they feel religiously inclined.

We made enquiries about rooms at the Master Builder's House before going down to the river, because now it is an hotel and we were looking for the perfect spot for a friend of ours to honeymoon in. Then we went through a gate and down to the bank near the little crazy pier.

A donkey with a keen taste for tobacco used to graze here and was, so they say, the first to welcome Queen Mary when not very long ago she honoured the Hard with a visit. I had hoped to make his acquaintance but there was no sign of life other than a poor bedraggled Skye terrier who was sitting alone in a canopied seat made from the bows of an old boat. I think she must have fallen off a sailing boat for she was very muddy and wet and was howling so dismally that it would have made an American saxophonist green with envy to hear her.

BUCKLER'S HARD

We went along a green stretch lit up by gorse in gorgeous bloom, past a cottage, under some handsome firs, skirted a spinney and a few fields, and reached Keeping Copse. At the gate we saw an apple tree in full blossom, and then a notice saying that game was preserved in the wood. Heaving a sigh I impressed upon Bill the necessity for keeping to the path and then, opening the gate, went into the wood.

Up till then we had had the river close at our side; now, though still our neighbour, it was not so near and screened from us by the oaks and hazels of one of the loveliest little greenwoods I know. Every part of the ground, barring the neat path running strictly straight ahead, was covered with green and enamelled with bright colours. Violets, wood anemonies, primroses, yellow pimpernel (absurdly early), and quantities of lungwort grew all together and crowded to the path's edge as if trying to make up to the walker for his being forbidden the joy of wandering about freely under the trees.

Oh, pheasant! pheasant!—but that is not fair and we will not say what we were going to because it is quite possible that save for the pheasant there would have been bungalows here instead of Keeping Copse. All the same we never see a game preserve or trespassing notice but we long to have the courage both to poach and trespass. Nearly everyone, I believe, feels the same; for though poaching as done by organised gangs with motor vans and nets is a hateful thing, there are very few of us who have not a soft spot for the fellow who by moonlight braves policeman, keeper, farmer, and landowner for the sake of something plump in fur or feather. I know of one hero who never sets a trap or fires a gun, yet keeps his larder stocked with game. His armoury consists of different sized catapults, the biggest capable of stunning a hare. They are good weapons for they are silent, and are deadly in the hands of a really good shot.

I suppose most country-bred children have done a bit of poaching; I know my uncles did. They took to the sport in the coverts of my grandfather's Suffolk parish and had, therefore, to be extra careful. To add to their difficulties my grandfather, who was an excellent shot, was great friends with the squire to whom the coverts belonged. But as they only poached because they wanted to feel they were ' living dangerously,' this knowledge added to my uncles' pleasure. One night they decided to try a roadside covert past which my grandfather and the squire would be walking after dining together. In a luckless moment they decided to post a sentry and chose my father, then a very little boy, for the duty. ' Hallie ' was immensely flattered that his big brothers should want him to come with them and determined to excel in what they had given him to do. Unfortunately he had a fatally wrong impression of what it was. He waited long and patiently in the chilly dusk on the covert's edge, straining his eyes for the first glimpse of his father, whispering the magic word his brothers had told him to say, over and over to himself. When at last he saw the tall, athletic figure of his father come striding round the bend of the road, the squire at his side, he rushed towards them, crying shrilly, ' Hullo, Daddy! Cave, Daddy! Cave,

cave ! It's all right Andoo, and Ermest, he's come ! ' The painful end of the story is best kept dark.

The path crossed a tiny railway line and came to the dilapidated buildings of the brickyard known as Bailey's Hard, and a thatched cottage with a garden full of flowers and fruit trees. Near the cottage is a stile and over it we climbed into a brilliant green field with trees all round and a patch of wood in the middle. Here Bill's self-control was strained almost to breaking point by the sight of fat, white-scutted brown forms bobbing away in all directions, and even Mr. Bundy had much ado to keep himself in hand. The path lies along the hedge to the right of the stile but is apparently so little used that it is practically invisible. It took us over a gate, across a stream in a wooded dip, up a green rise marred by a boggy bit, then over another gate into a field where the river came into view again beyond a fence all pink and white with wild apple blossom. Two more fields we crossed without losing touch with the river and then, over a last gate, went down an alley from where, over apple blossom and through elm trunks, we saw the stone gatehouse and ruined walls of Beaulieu Abbey.

I suppose everyone who comes to Beaulieu knows its Abbey's history—how it was founded by King John in 1205 for the Cistercians whose wont it was to choose some remote place near wood, water, and grassland. How its founder never lived to see its dedication, which was made splendid by the attendance of Henry the Third and his court and the bishops of Exeter, Chichester, Bath, and Winchester, the latter performing the ceremony. How it flourished and grew strong and added farmlands to itself, and how it afforded sanctuary to the Countess of Warwick after the King Maker had fallen in battle, and to Perkin Warbeck. How at last, when it went the way of all monasteries under Henry the Eighth, much of its stone was used for the building of the stubby fortresses of Calshot and Hurst. Its monks were scattered and fled none knows where and its abbot, Thomas Stevens, by dint of licking Cromwell's shoes, received the living of Bentley. The account I like best of all those I have read is in Elizabeth Croly's *Lure of the New Forest*. It is brief, full of meat, and tells all sorts of moving things about those sorry times when abbey after beautiful abbey fell because a king was tired of his wife and his chief officer fell because he badgered his royal master into marriage with an ugly woman.

The ruins are beautiful and are so lovingly kept that it was devastating to find in the village church metal text-bearing labels nailed round the thirteenth-century arches. The church was once the monks' refectory and is famous for its hanging stone pulpit reached by a vaulted, arcaded stairway contained in the thickness of the wall.

In the Abbey museum the thing which appealed to me most was the double heart coffin. It is cut out of a small block of stone and has two round hollows in it and a plain stone lid. It is believed to have held the hearts of King John's son Richard, Earl of Cornwall, and of his third wife, 'the gem of women,' Beatrice de Falkenstein, niece of the Archbishop of Cologne.

As we wandered about the village I thought not of the Montagus who live in Palace House and are lords of the manor, nor of the abbots of Beaulieu, but of W. H. Hudson, who said of it that it 'has a distinction above all Hampshire villages and is unlike all others in its austere beauty and atmosphere of old-world seclusion and quietude.'

We looked across a mere at the Montagus' house, which is built on to the abbots' great gatehouse ; at the pool near the church where the monks kept their carp ; and at the old mill-house on the edge of the salt-water basin into which the river widens before the ruins. It was in this tree-hung lake that Hudson saw a swallow, dipping to skim a fly off the surface, leapt at and all but seized by a big pike.

We went back to Buckler's Hard by the narrow road that winds up the hill and, passing the stone barns of Beufre, where once the abbotorial oxen stood, runs on between copses and fields where now great coppery pheasants stalk among the bright green young corn and across which we thought the russet roofs of Buckler's Hard showed almost at their best.

II

One of the nicest things about the Forest is that it always seems to comfort you with something rare or charming if you lose yourself. Our next walk from Buckler's Hard was an example of this.

We started at about two o'clock in the afternoon of a summer's day and went along the river's edge through Keeping Copse to Beaulieu, and there turned up the road running between the Abbey and Palace House.

At first the road rose steadily through a few grass fields and then, on entering Great Goswell Copse, began to dive and rear like a monstrous switchback railway. Undistressed by the sharp rises and sudden falls because we were able to go our own pace, we found them delightful for from each summit and from every dip we caught lovely glimpses of this enchanting wood whose trees grow on ground as tumbled as a fever-patient's bed and where bluebells and may trees make the air sweet.

In spite of notices saying ' private road to Harford House,' and one or two other houses whose names I forget, we pressed on undismayed because the old man at the Abbey ticket office had beamingly encouraged us to go ahead without fear, only warning me to keep ' they liddle dogs ' on their leashes because of the game.

Nearly a mile from the wood's beginning we came on a regular Etoile of paths with a clump of bushes in the centre as its Arc de Triomphe. Midway between two of these paths was a notice saying that one of them was the private road to Harford House, but which of the pair it referred to it did not state. A lucky choice took us up the left path, which ran under seedy pines, past a villa, and then led us through a gate on to Beaulieu Hilltop Heath.

After the cool of the wood it was terrific coming out on to this unshadowed upland where the colour of the gorse was dazzling, its scent overpowering, and not a cloud was aloft to temper the sun to the unshorn pedestrian.

A rough track all sand and heather brought us clear of the wood's left wing and gave us an unexpected and beautiful glimpse of the tree-clothed hills of Denny Lodge Walk. After crossing a wider track punched with the blunt little hoof-prints of sheep and tagged with their wool we headed over the heath towards the scarlet, distant brick of Dibden Purlieu, skirting a tempting greenwood on the way and passing close against two barrows.

If Hudson had filled my mind in Beaulieu, here on Hilltop Heath he seemed to walk at our side. Of all the passages I love in *Hampshire Days* the ones which move me most are those describing the hours he spent sitting on a barrow here in the failing light of a cold and windy June evening. He loved the Forest and longed to lie up here on Hilltop ' to have always about me that wildness which I best loved—the rude incult heath, the beautiful desolation ; to have harsh furze and ling and bramble and bracken to grow on me, and only wild creatures for visitors and company. The little stonechat, the tinkling meadowpipit, the excited whitethroat to sing to me in summer ; the deep-burrowing rabbit to bring down his warmth and familiar smell among my bones ; the heat-loving adder, rich in colour, to find when summer is gone a dry safe shelter and hibernaculum in my empty skull.'

And then as the stars came out his thoughts turned to the men who lie in the barrows and he says, '. . . they were with me in the twilight on the barrow in crowds, sitting and standing in groups, and many lying on their sides on the turf below, their heads resting on their hands. They, too, all had their faces turned towards Beaulieu. Evening by evening for many and many a century they had looked to that point, towards the black wood on the horizon, where there were people and sounds of human life. Day by day for centuries they had listened with wonder and fear to the Abbey bells, and to the distant chanting of the monks. And the Abbey has been in ruins for centuries, open to the sky and overgrown with ivy; but still towards that point they look with apprehension, since men still dwell there, strangers to them, the little busy eager people, hateful in their artificial indoor lives, who do not know and who care nothing for them, who worship not and fear not the dead that are underground, but dig up their sacred places and scatter their bones and ashes, and despise and mock them because they are dead and powerless.

' It is not strange that they fear and hate. I look at them—their dark, pale, furious faces—and think that if they could be visible thus in the daylight, all who came to that spot or passed near it would turn and fly with a terrifying image in their mind which would last to the end of life.'

Fortunately the threatening legions were invisible when we came and we felt no hostility quivering over the white-hot air towards us from the barrows. Possibly this was because we have the same dislike for the disinterring of human bones and the robbing of their graves as Hudson had. It is a pastime which must surely only appeal to those whose curiosity is their chief characteristic, or whose love of museum knowledge has calloused their natural respect for the dead. Yet Walter Scott is said to have been the first to ravage a New Forest gravemound.

192

There are more barrows on Beaulieu's two heaths than anywhere else in the Forest, fifty-four being, I believe, the exact number. These mounds are not called barrows locally, as I learned on asking a labourer to direct me to some a little while back. ' Barrows ? ' he said puzzledly ; and then with a sudden lightening of countenance, ' Oh, you means *rabbit burrows* ! Yes, yes, there's a-plenty of they up there.' The correct Hampshire name for them is ' butt.'

A mile covered, we found ourselves at the highway's edge and saw the track to the Noads running off left-handed, back into the heather again. We could have reached the track without coming as far as the Dibden road but so many other paths run over the moor, any of which we might have mistaken for the path we wanted, that we decided on the fool-proof course of following our original track to its bitter end, as where it stops the Noad's track begins.

The glaring white gravel path went fairly straight at first, then passing between two gravel pits curved away to the left and dropped into a winding, deep runway with young silver birches growing on its heathered banks.

The path chose a green patch with a yew and some holly and thorn bushes growing in it as the most suitable place to negotiate the trough, and here we lay down in the shade for a while. Some mares and foals were grazing in the bottom, and alone on the slope stood a donkey. We felt sorry for him, thinking his more graceful cousins had ostracized him, until catching sight of a brown stallion coming down into the bottom he pricked his long ears and trotted towards the little horse, to be welcomed with an affectionate whinny. Together they wandered off to feed at a comfortable distance from the women and children, and we realised that it had been a sense of his superiority which had kept him aloof.

The Noads are a green and pleasant fraternity of little woods. They grow on the slope of the heath and look over the stark basin called Dibden Bottom to lovely wild country where moors melt into woods and hills rise in sylvan tiers as far as eye can see.

We followed the path through one of the woods, at whose entrance stood a troop of young birches. Blackbirds and finches sang in the weather-pruned branches of the short oaks and sulphur butterflies gleamed against the dark trunks of the yews as we passed under the cool green alleyway. We came out to find ourselves at the top of a steep little hill, where we tarried to enjoy the view, and then descending between golden gorse bushes kept left along the bottom of the hill, through the fringe of another Noad, and crossed a heathery bit into King's Hat Enclosure. On this heath sundew spreads its sticky fingers for the unwary flies, and prepared us for the spongy places we found in our way. These we got over without trouble, however, because of the freshly felled young pine trees lying about in hundreds. They made excellent bridges besides filling the air with their keen, sweet scent.

Though pines darken the gate into King's Hat Enclosure they soon give way and the wood becomes a pleasant blend of oaks, yews, and hollies; bluebells with great courage have won themselves a footing here too, in spite of
194

bramble and bracken. Sweet chestnuts grace the gateway on to the tarmac road which comes up from Beaulieu to cross Dibden Bottom, wander along the Forest boundary, and leave it near Colbury.

Close to this gate is a small cottage with an orchard, a paddock, and a few crazy sheds of such primitive appearance that they look as if Gurth the Swineherd might have been their contemporary. We found no one at home, the kennel even was empty, and only a few fowls were there to keep an eye on the place. We discovered the owners sitting in the sun on some pine-trunks which were lying by the roadside waiting to be carried away. They were mother, two fat little boys, and Pongo, a rough-haired terrier ; father was away at work.

I asked mother for directions and information and, having received encouraging replies, fell into talk with her about the children. She said the youngest was only two years old but the eldest one was four and would, she supposed, have to start school next year. There being nothing but woods and moors to be seen up and down the road, which was long and straight, I asked her to which village he would be going. She replied that he would have to walk to Beaulieu three miles away and supposed that he would be all right as ' other children did it,' but she looked uncertainly from him to a large petrol lorry that went roaring past as she spoke. This compulsory education was, of course, a good thing she remarked, but getting the children to school was often a big problem to those parents whose little ones had long distances to walk and whose cottages did not lie in the way of the buses or cabs sent out by the authorities to collect 'long distance scholars.' In her own case she had to decide whether her small son was to walk his daily six miles to school alone along a road where swift traffic was fairly frequent, or whether she should take him and fetch him on her bicycle, which not only meant twelve miles a day for her, but also leaving the baby in the cottage with only Pongo to guard it.

Pongo she said she had saved from drowning, a fate to which he had been condemned because his owner had no use for a rickety puppy. His new mistress carried him home, bandaged his tiny twisted legs, fed him up and nursed him till he got over his weakness and turned into the sturdy chap he is to-day. It was because of Pongo, who took to circling Bill with a truculent look in his eye and mutterings in his throat, that we cut our conversation short and said goodbye.

A few yards down the road in the direction of Beaulieu we came across the path we wanted. The map showed it plainly as running through the trees over the way, crossing the stream under their branches and mounting the moor beyond, turning sharply right and reaching another road just below Ipley Manor, having skirted the trees and passed between a chain of four ponds.

We were soon across the heather and under the trees which arch the stream and follow it for some distance. Here we came suddenly to a green glade with a lily pool under an oak. The stream (given as a mere trickle on the map) went twisting swiftly past, deep and wide, with ferns and kingcups on its low banks and wild iris already three

196

feet high standing in its shallows. The lilies were golden, the grass vividly green and brightly sprinkled with eye-bright and daisies, betony, and moneywort ; at the foot of the oak a briar and a bramble were entwined. An exquisite little place, far more lovely than Queen's Bower because it is apparently unknown and is therefore unspoilt. The dogs loved it as much as I did ; Bill dived into the stream after anything I chose to throw and Mr. Bundy paddled as energetically as it is possible to paddle.

A tree-trunk and an ancient beam lashed together for a bridge took us over the stream and into the moor track. Here we saw that all was not well, for instead of clinging to the trees the track climbed the moor's flank, going straight ahead with no suggestion of a leaning to the right. Moreover, there was only one pond in sight and that was close at hand on the left and had no path leading to it.

We searched carefully for the track to the four linked pools but after a while came to the conclusion that it must have got drowned by the bog glistening all round us, or smothered by the alders lining the moor side of the stream's avenue.

Before turning back we thought it wise to try the main track in case it later developed a side path which might yet lead us to the pools and get us over the bog. The moor is small but its charm is great, for it is ringed by the green crests of North Gate, Culverly, and Fernycroft woods, is deep in heather and clear of pinelets, and stands above a valley bog where many coloured waterplants, alders, and a few pine trees grow.

We had only gone a few yards when we heard a feathery whispering overhead and, looking up quickly, saw two big white birds with dark heads and long outstretched necks. They swept past us, skimmed low over the edge of the moor, and disappeared. This, we knew, meant that water lay near, for though we had not recognised the actual breed of the birds, we realised they were some kind of duck or goose.

The breeze which had sprung up was blowing towards us so we thought it was worth while trying to get near enough to the birds to find out what they were. Extraordinary luck was ours. Not only were there two white shapes on the pond when we caught sight of it, but several ponies were crackling and splashing about among the alders at one end of it and in the middle of the little trail descending the slope, right on the water's lip, stood a bushy young pine. With the noise of the ponies to drown any clumsiness of approach, with the pine to screen us and the breeze to carry our scent away, we had everything in our favour, but all the same it was an anxious journey. At any moment a pheasant or partridge might whirr up from the heather and give the alarm, or a pony might sight us in turning his head to nip a fly off his ribs, or the birds might swim clear of the tree. Mercifully none of these things happened and we reached the pine without betraying our presence.

Here indeed was cause to stand and stare and, leaning against the rough little trunk and peering through the fuzzy branches, I gave myself up to the blissful rite. The pond was bright blue, its surface teased by the light wind into tiny waves ; on two sides were the green, and gold, and purple moorland slopes ; at one end a cloud of alders shut out the trees, at the other the bog entered, meandering down between the heather, tufted with trees and full of flowers. All this was lovely, but it was as nothing compared with the beauty of the birds gently rocking on the water.

I am very ignorant about birds, only being able to tell the more boldly marked among the less common species, but these I recognised at once as shell-duck. In Suffolk I often saw them on the river mudflats when sailing with my father, but never before had I been so near to them as now. Their heads are blunt and richly, deeply green ; their bills are coral ; their flight and tail feathers are coal black ; they wear chestnut bibs and their legs are pink ; yet at a distance they seem white and black, and when they flew over us on the moor they had looked like snow.

An old groom at Lyndhurst told me that they nest in rabbit holes and that he has actually seen the birds removing the rightful owners should the poor rabbits object to leaving. He said, too, that in wet years, when the burrows in the wilder parts have been flooded, the shell-duck have been known to occupy runs as near the town as Bolton's Bench.

Our brace were enjoying themselves so much, and were making such happy little intimate chuckings and low bubbling whistles, that we tried to steal away without disturbing them. But they must have caught sight of us, or else something else disturbed them, for they suddenly flashed over us again and held the air for as long as we were on the moor.

On our way back to the track we noticed a large stone surrounded by iron railings, and on going up to it read the cheering reminder that in the midst of life we are in death, and on the other side saw the badge of the New Forest foxhounds. The writing below said that the stone marks the place where a Mr. Carter was thrown and killed whilst hunting with the pack.

The farther along the track we went the more painfully clear it became that we were going wrong. Our constant expeditions down narrow trails only brought us to the wrong side of the bog, and, try as we might, we could find no passage through it which Mr. Bundy and I could manage, though Bill forded it two or three times and became in consequence as spotted and blotched as a Chinese circus pony.

There was only one thing to do, and that was to return to the bridge and the lily pool and from there make our way along the tedious tarmac until we picked up the footpath we had hoped to join below Ipley Manor, where it crossed the road and entered Dibden Bottom.

As it happened we were able to save ourselves a good bit of road walking because we found that a path went from the lily pond and, keeping under the trees, followed the stream for quite a nice distance. Then it left the trees and crawled so undecidedly up the rising heath that we were about to leave it for the road when we saw the track we had been looking for running across it not far ahead.

Soon we were over the tarmac and following the sandy heather-ridged track across Dibden Bottom. It took us gradually uphill, toiling through young pines whose stems were blackened and whose needles had been dyed red by a recent fire, past alders and bogs where dark little marsh birds darted about and from whence we heard the snort of a startled snipe on her hidden nest. Kings Hat lay below on the right, the moor ran up on the left, ahead rose a high bluff pricked out with gorse and dark with heather, and to the right of it hung the Noads.

The sun was sinking, dark clouds were rising to meet it, the land was turning gloomy and the air growing colder when we began our ascent of the bluff. We climbed slowly, unspurred by anticipation, for we thought we knew all that lay before us—the houses of the Purlieu and the darkening moor. We were quite unprepared for what the bluff had in store for us.

When we had gained the summit there were the houses and the heath sure enough, but over the trees on the left, with a background of packed roofs, towering chimneys, derricks and cranes and smoke, we saw the scarlet funnels of a liner and knew we were looking at Southampton Docks. It all looked so startlingly close that we wondered why none of the noises of that busy land should have come to us.

A road runs alongside the Purlieu, past gorse hedges and may hedges neatly trimmed and sheltered by laburnams and lilacs. Where the tarmac crooks sharply to the left we took to a gravel road and left it almost immediately for a path going right-handed over the heath.

The path is carried on a bank and goes along by an alder-filled bog, where a brace of snipe, a few plover, and some small, swift brown birds were drumming, crying, and skimming about. It dips through two wet bits, each with a pond; one pond is dull and green, the other so full of the fluffy pink and white bog bean that it looks as though the top of a submerged orchard had broken through the water and burst into blossom. At the cost of wet shoes and stained stockings I picked a few bog bean heads and found one of them to be two and a half inches long.

We saw barrows on our left, woods all round, heard a late lark and cuckoos calling, and recognised the downs of the Isle of Wight above the trees. It was after seven o'clock, we were pleasantly tired and had the whole moors to ourselves. When a gravel track cut across our path we followed it right-handed and were taken down to the bog. It, too, was beautiful with bog bean, was threaded by a clear stream, and lay between high banks where heather and young gorse grew sparsely on the white gravel. We crossed by means of a bridge made of a stove pipe, an iron bedstead and turfs, and then followed tracks through the heather until we gained the cross-roads above Beaulieu. It was nearly dark when we reached the village and through Keeping Copse we could scarcely see our way.

202

CHAPTER XII

SALTMARSHES AND THE COUNTRY NORTH OF BEAULIEU

Two or three extraordinarily happy years spent on the coast of Suffolk instilled in my childish heart a love for the open marshlands which so often accompany a river to its meeting with the sea, and that love has never lessened but has lasted with me to this day.

It was then, with a feeling of exultation, that I discovered in examining the map for the whereabouts of St. Leonards Grange and Bergerie that these old farmsteads of Beaulieu's monks stood above a goodly acreage of saltmarshes. Moreover, I saw at a glance that it would be an easy matter to map out a walk which would take us right round the marshes and include not only Bergerie and St. Leonards but Sowley Pond as well.

Exactly opposite Buckler's Hard is a road going almost straight to St. Leonards where there is a mighty barn, one of the largest in England, and the ruins of a beautiful little chapel. This we took early one sunny morning in June when there was a light east wind blowing to keep things cool. We found the road friendly to foot passengers, for its flowery hedges were low enough to allow us to look over them with ease at the prosperous fields, distant woods, and the red brick walls and golden lichened roofs of Clobb Farm's barns and byres. An elm as graceful as a green fountain grew at the farm gate, and a little further on through a gap in the trees on our left I caught a misty glimpse of the Island. Pheasants crouched in the corn, fat thrushes hopped about among the cattle on the grassland, and a redshank surprised us by his sudden appearance overhead. Not a car disturbed the morning.

As it enters a copse the road swings to the right, goes sharply up and down and stops dead, decapitated by the Beaulieu-St. Leonards road. We turned left for St. Leonards, and clear of the copse saw over the rough hedges now lining the way marshy fields filled with sedge and reeds. This meant, we knew, that the river was not far away and the redshank's appearance was explained.

Almost at once we came upon St. Leonards. Though in ruins the barn is stupendous. In its prime it was sixty feet high, seventy-seven feet wide, two hundred and twenty-six feet long, and could hold nearly all the crops of the abbey's lands immediately surrounding it. One gable end is flush with the road and towers above the elms growing close on either side of it like living buttresses.

The chapel ruins are in the garden of the Grange, a charming old house. The owners were away when we arrived, but the gardener said he was sure they would not mind if he took me to see the chapel. It is a beautiful little place with handsome tracery in its windows, the remains of lovely niches and a good doorway. Flowers grow wherever they can find root-hold among its stones and it is approached through a perfect rock garden.

The gardener said that there was an underground passage from the Grange to Beaulieu Abbey, but no one knows now where the entrance to it lies. In his grandfather's youth it was possible to get into the passage from an opening down by the river, and the old man told him that when a lad he and a party of his more adventurous friends tried to explore it, using this way in. They had to go by boat because the tunnel was half-full of water and they carried candles because it was as dark as night. However, they were forced to turn back before they had gone very far as the foul air first turned the candle flames an unhealthy blue then extinguished them altogether, and finally began to make the explorers feel very bad themselves. No one tried to better their effort, and when they died there was nobody left who even knew where the river entrance was.

The road curls round the barns on its way to Bergerie and Sowley, and just where it bends the lane to the marshes runs off on the left.

The lane goes downhill between fields and tangled high hedges out of which grow wind-trimmed oaks and elegant ash trees curiously untouched by the weather's rough handling. In a grassy ditch Bill disturbed a pheasant and her brood. The bird behaved with great courage, tumbling in the dust a few yards away from our feet until all the young birds had whirred away ; then she rose like a rocket and was soon out of sight. When I looked at Bill I saw that for reasons known only to himself he was standing stock still with tightly closed eyes.

At the end of the lane is a gate and a pond sheltered by elms and overhung by a rose bush. I think it will always stay clear in my memory, for as I opened the gate a whole flock of goldfinches rose twittering from its shallows and darting through the trees went curtseying away over the fields.

In front of us lay the saltmarshes, cut by dikes into paddocks where glossy cart-horses and pied cows were grazing in the sun.

The lane here became a track with a hedge on one side, a stream and the marshes on the left, and ran straight down to Gins, one of the many farmsteads which I want to buy. It is L-shaped and of mellow brick, its outbuildings lie close against it; at the back is an orchard of old trees, to right and left are the open saltmarshes, and close behind it the river, sternly shorn of all its sylvan graces, goes manfully down to its sea death.

The farmer's wife was most friendly, and when I admired her house insisted on taking me inside and showing me the age-blackened beams in some of the cool low rooms, and the original oak floorboards, very wide and held in place by handforged nails, in others. She was intrigued with Mr. Bundy, and told me she had eleven cats besides the three dogs I had seen leashed to table legs in separate rooms. The dogs were thus confined on account of game, she said, and warned me to keep Bill at heel when I got on to the marshes, because the shooting was in the hands of some ' majors and colonels ' who had taken the old coastguard cottages at Needs Oar Point.

This information was a blow, for though in possession of quite charming uncles of this species, I have in my time come up against the peppery, red-faced, pop-eyed variety which furiously addresses you as Madam, and informs you in a voice trembling with rage that you are trespassing, or that your doomed and unattractive dog has snaffled its golf ball. However, I do not believe in crossing bridges before coming to them, so I resolutely put the military gentlemen out of my mind and refused to allow any thought of them to spoil the glorious three-quarters of a mile which lay between their cottages at Needs Oar Point and Gins.

At the stile behind Gins we paused to look back along the river to where against the last of the oakwoods the masts of distant yachts rose above golden reed-beds. Then we set off along the low, broad sea-wall running straight ahead to Needs Oar Point.

On our left the river glittered wide and sweet smelling, deserted except for one small yacht on whose deck a stalwart in dark jersey and sea-boots stumped about with a clanking pail. Ahead were the grand lines of the heat-misted Island showing over the colonels' and majors' cottages. To the right stretched away the saltmarshes bounded by far-away woods, their long grasses rippling under the breeze, their dikes and pools flashing defiance to the thirsty sun. From the river came only the noise of lapping water, an occasional cry of a gull, and the sounds the sailor made about his work. From the marshes we heard curlew, plover, redshank, and the distant bleating of sheep.

Before we reached the cottages we had passed by two ponds. One was small and had two wild swans on its banks and a redshank standing knee-deep in its shallows, the other was much larger, and several swans, dark little wild-duck and many redshanks idled about its tufted inlets.

The river turns away from the cottages and a gorse-covered bank stands up in front of them. We negotiated an awkward gate hung on a bridge over a deep channel, and running over the springy turf mounted the bank and got the surprise of our lives. Shining and dancing in the sun, and only separated from us by a few insignificant mudflats, was the Solent. The Island looked so close we could hardly believe it was really three miles away, even though the haze made it impossible to distinguish houses or trees.

Ringed plovers, looking devastating in their dark masks and bibs, ran about the mudflats on spidery legs, whistling to themselves while they hunted for food ; baby rabbits, made bold by the number of funk-holes at their disposal, led the dogs on wild chases among the gorse bushes. On a sudden we heard a harsh protest from the clouds and looking up saw a long way off a flock of gulls mobbing a heron. The screaming and wailing of the gulls came faintly on the wind, and every now and then the heron sounded his angry note as he strove to out-distance them. The group made me think of an airship being attacked by hostile airplanes, so slow and laborious was the one, so nimble and swift were the others.

When the birds had disappeared inland we turned our attention to the path, and saw with a shock that not only did it run through the wired enclosure surrounding the cottages but passed right under their seaward windows. These windows being open indicated that the occupants were at home, which caused us a further sinking of heart. Fixing the leads to the dogs' collars and putting on a bold front I led the way through the gate and approached the cottages, composing haughty rejoinders to imaginary attacks and practising what I hoped were aloof and chilly facial expressions.

Directly we reached the little houses I realised we need have had no qualms. Under each window was a tiny garden far too charming to have been made by the owner of a savage heart. All had gay colours and sweet scents, and one was given character by Purbeck stone and a lily pond, about the size of a card table, filled with pink and white waterlilies.

Not a soul was about, so we went unaccosted through another gate on to a gravel road, which we left again almost at once to dive under some wire and take to a well-defined footpath running over the turf above the Solent's edge and heading straight for a bungalow.

Untidy hedges, rough fields, and stunted oaks shut off the marshes on our right, and a little farther inland we saw the old red roofs of Warren farm. Though we missed the marshes we found the walking good, for the turf twinkled with thousands of seapinks, and in the shelter of the gorse bushes grew the lovely little cream-coloured briar with apple-scented leaves which we had first met growing on a Dorset heath.

When we reached the bungalow an outburst of yapping greeted us as two little border terriers came charging out through the French windows and tore back and forth yelling battle, murder, and sudden death at us through the close-meshed wire fence. The outcry drew their mistress' attention from her book and brought her down to the fence, where she stayed to make love to Mr. Bundy and to admire Bill, who she said ' *must* be a lady with a face like that '; he certainly was simpering abominably.

From this delightful lady I learned that my golden

briar is called the burnet rose, and that the bronzed and
hearty fellow I could see cutting ' vuzz ' behind the house
was the proud father of twenty-eight children ! She also
told me that she comes to the bungalow every summer for
peace and quiet, and that it is impossible to be lonely
there because, though she is practically neighbourless,
the Solent is never without traffic for long. ' As you see,
now,' she laughed, and looking westward I saw a tramp
steamer coming up in a cloud of brown smoke, and east-
ward was in time to watch a mighty liner turning slowly
and grandly into Southampton Water.

In Cowes week there is a lot to look at from the bungalow garden as the yachts often turn nearly opposite it
and come quite close in shore. Once the ' Britannia ' sailed
so near that the watchers could see the king quite plainly
looking at something through his binoculars and laughing
at what he saw.

Bidding our friend goodbye we continued our way
along the path, and skirting some wild ground which once
was a golf links came to a stile, beyond which was a sea-
wall path and another grand expanse of marshes. At the
end of the sea-wall were the trees and bungalows of Little-
marsh. From this stile we saw a marvellous sight. A
big pond sprawled anyhow among reed-tufts and sedgy
creeks a little way beyond the dike at the sea-wall's foot,
and dozing on its banks, floating on its waters or standing
stiffly in its shallows, we counted nine shell-duck, as well
as dozens of redshank and wild-duck.

On turning away from the pond we were confronted
with a humorous but rather agitating spectacle. Gallop-

ing towards us, tails in air, along the top of the sea-wall, were a herd of cows, who were varying their gait with bucks and bellowings.   Some horses, up till then grazing peacefully in the marshes, hearing the noise of the horned ballet, flung up their heads and heels, raced to the dike, leapt it, and thundered on to the sea-wall.   Their arrival sent the cows clumsily down the opposite side, over the shingle and into the sea.   The horses followed them, and all came to rest up to their bodies in the water and out of reach of the torturing flies which had set them off.

Having assured ourselves that the animals had really settled down we hastened along the path to Little Marsh, and when we got there went down to some waterlogged clay diggings, the dogs to drink and I to watch the graceful manœuvrings of the fat-bodied vividly powder-blue dragonflies skimming over the yellow surface.

Because the bungalow gardens come right down to the beach comfortable walking ends at Little Marsh, as the sand is loose and dusty and cut by innumerable break-waters.   Some of the breakwaters are made of round up-rights bleached silver by the sun and salt winds, and are so sloped that they resemble giant panpipes ; others are hung with bladder wrack and make one think of corded poodles.   But though the actual going was heavy there was much to enjoy.   Where sand mingled with shingle and turf at the bungalow fences we saw growing juicy-leaved sea plants and lovely yellow hornpoppies sticking out their long green tongues ; escorted by a seaplane another liner came by, making the Island ' a very little thing ' ; and suddenly from the long grass of a neglected garden

212

flashed a shell-duck, its breast golden with the sunny glow from the sand, its colours bright. In another garden were some old ships' figureheads, leaning towards the sea as though they yearned to be driving out across it again and were sick to death of their earthly moorings.

When the bungalows ended at last fields took their place, and squeezed in between the sand and the ragged bushes, huge mulleins, and purple teazles of their fences we found a narrow path. To Bill the last three-quarters of a mile had not mattered so much because he had been bouncing along in the sea, but to Mr. Bundy and me it had been rather tiring and we hailed the path with a cheer.

Another half-mile brought us to where some men were putting the finishing touches to a whitewashed, red-roofed cottage, beside which a green path divided into sections by sunk balks of timber, ran inland. The men told us we should come out opposite Sowley Pond if we followed the path to its end, but if we wanted to keep along by the sea a bit longer there was another lane a good mile farther on.

I thought Mr. Bundy had had as much of sand walking as was good for him, so we went up the path and through an iron gate under some bushes into a lane kept cool and delicious by tall trees and hedges. It wound on past a house with poplars in its garden, a lonely lot of hen houses, a nearly dry stream, and then confronted us with a terribly respectable white gate. On the gate leaned a burly man in the decent garb of a squire's employee. He was watching us approach with the awful calm worn

213

by keepers or farmers waiting for the trespasser who has no way of escape open to him other than that of ignoble and hasty retreat.

Fortified by the knowledge that by some miraculous chance both dogs were walking sedately to heel when we hove in sight I put on what I hoped was an innocent air and asked him politely if he could tell us where we were.

' On private praarpity,' he replied, grinning affably, ' and you gets off it through this yere gate, what its my duty to open to such as you what comes up from the beach and don't know as you're trespassing, and to shut it against them as comes along the road and don't know no better than to come pushing through in spite of the notice.'

He was a good, civil creature, told me that the trees in front hid Sowley Pond, and said I had better keep the dogs on their leads as all the land from here to Beaulieu was preserved. Noticing that his eyes were fixed on Bill's bleeding tongue, and realising the futility of trying to convince him that the blood was not newly wrung from a hare or rabbit but due to a bramble scratch, I hastily said goodbye and made off towards Sowley Pond.

It is a large and very lovely pool lying behind the roadside and encircled by trees. In the old days it supplied fish for the abbey stewponds, and then was called South Legh; it had other names as well which sound much better—Colgrimesmore and Frieswater. Grand names, tasting of ancient pre-Christian Britain perhaps, for it is an easy step from Frieswater to Freya's water.

214

Later on an ironworks, whose great hammer was heard all over the Forest when the south-westerly wind blew, grew up on its banks. Now, fortunately, all trace of these works is hidden, and only the saying ' There will be rain when Sowley hammer is heard ' lives to keep them in mind.

Much of the ironstone brought to the works was washed up on the coast, ' particularly the coast of Beauley manor,' and it is said that such was the demand for the ore that even the wheat harvesting would be forsaken if news of a lot of ocean-delivered ironstone reached the farmer's ears.

There is a path to the pond's edge, and as we went down it a terrifying din broke out—roarings, coughings, and barkings the like of which I had never heard before. Hurrying to the pond, and looking across it in the direction from which the noise was coming, I was just in time to see a heron drop down into the crests of some fir trees and remembered that there was a heronry here.

There was no way round the water's edge by which we could reach the fir trees so we went back to the road in search of another path, hoping to find one leading straight to the herony. Paths there were, but as the mouth of each was stopped with game notices we had to go our way, and added another charming lieu to our list of lovely places closed to such as we for the pheasant's sake.

As we went sadly along by the trees screening the pond from the road a squirrel darted out of the grass and started to race up a pine trunk. Finding that we meant him no harm he stopped when still only a few feet from the

215

ground, and spinning round hung head downwards ready
to leap to the ground again directly we were out of the
way.

From the pond onwards we knew we had only road
walking before us, but this did not depress us, the hedges
were so lovely with wild roses and honeysuckle, the
ditches frothy with kex, the elder bushes were laden with
blossom and the brambles with their lilac flowers. Everywhere we looked we saw young healthy crops and folk at
work among them, or fresh green pasture with contented
cattle dozing in the shade of their hedges and great trees,
and there was not a single car about.

At the first cross-roads we came to we turned to the
right and came at the end of half a mile to the poplar
guarded red farmstead marking the site of the abbey's
sheep farm and bearing to this day its name of Bergerie.
The roofs of house and buildings were covered like those
of Clobb Farm with brilliant golden lichen. A mile more
and we were passing St. Leonards again and here I
turned my back while the dogs waded in and drank of
the odoriferous and inky waters of the roadside pond,
unable to deny them such cooling refreshment and equally
unable to watch them at it.

II

Our encounter with the keeper, mild as it was, and our
disappointment in finding that Sowley Pond was not for
the likes of us, made us decide against any more walks in
the neighbourhood of private property and the pheasant.
This self-banishment was no hardship, for we had all the

country between Beaulieu and Lyndhurst open to us and knew it to be of the kind we loved—varied, beautiful, free, and the home of all kinds of wild things.

As a jumping-off place I decided on Pig Bush, which is marked on the map as being about three miles north of Beaulieu on the road to Lyndhurst.

I do not know how the place got its name. It may be that some porcine tragedy was enacted here, or perhaps it was thus christened to commemorate a brilliant exploit of the celebrated pig belonging to the Mr. Toomers.

This pig was a most amazing person and has rightly been honoured by both pen and brush. In 1807 *Rural Sports* published an account of her doings, of which the following is an extract:

' Of this most extraordinary Animal will be here stated a short History, to the Veracity of which there are hundreds of living Witnesses. Slut was bred in the New Forest and trained by Mr Richard Toomer and Mr Edward Toomer, to find, point and retrieve, Game as well as the best Pointer; her Nose was superior to any Pointer they ever possessed, and no two men in England

217

had better. Slut has stood Partridges, Black-game, Pheasants, Snipes and Rabbits in the same day, but was never known to point a Hare. When called to go out shooting, she would come home off the Forest at full Stretch, and be as elevated as a dog upon being shown the gun.'

At Brockenhurst her portrait hangs in a handsome frame in the Olde Tea House, whose proprietor is Mr. C. H. Toomer, a descendant of her owners. She is shown gazing fixedly and open-mouthed at a sitting bird in a New Forest glade, a handsome black creature with white ankle-socks and a long hairy tail.

I do not know whether she ever had any family of her own, but if she did none of her offspring seem to have inherited her gifts. Probably she died childless, preferring the pleasures of the chase to the duties of domesticity.

My mother is devoted to pigs, and once had three little sows called Sophia, Gertrude, and Maud. Maud got her name because she would come into the garden, Sophia and Gertrude she christened after a friend and herself. These pigs, she declared, were as intelligent and charming as dogs, had the most amiable dispositions, and were even fonder of her than she of them. They used to follow her on her country walks, and when she sat down to rest would group themselves gracefully about her, only rising when she did though the grass near them might be littered with acorns.

When they grew up the first tragedy of their lives took place. Poor Sophia died in childbed, leaving a large family of little black satin orphans. The noble, big-hearted Gertrude had successfully come through her own ordeal and now undertook to rear Sophia's offspring as well as her own, which she did to admiration. However, when her next family arrived she refused to have anything to do with them! The second tragedy came when my father decided to go up to London to live, and the little Devonshire farm had to be sold. Maud and Gertrude, mother had to admit, were not cut out for London life, and so homes were found for them where they would have the run of orchard and fields, spotless pens, and, she was assured, a death due to old age or brought on by over-feeding.

While on the subject of pigs it might be as well to mention that the big, jetty pigs of the New Forest are said to owe their existence to some boars and sows brought from Germany by Charles the First. I discovered this and the rather nerve-racking information that they are ' as fierce at heart as any old boar of the German forests ' from the Crespigny and Hutchinson book about the Forest. Pigs when ill used, and sometimes when they have just farrowed, can be very savage I know. Our old nurse, who revelled in the gruesome, told us about a little girl who had her leg bitten off by a rampageous sow and my sister has been introduced to a mighty white sow who was actually said to be a murderess and owed her continued existence solely to her illustrious ancestry.

Once on Castle Top at Burley I saw an amusing sight. A groom, trying hard to appear dignified and unconcerned, was keeping his horse going just sufficiently fast to out-distance a couple of white pigs ardently and noisily pursuing it ; they were bumping into each other like grey-hounds jockeying for position on the track and coming along at a really round pace. I think they were in high good-humour but, of course, on the other hand they might have had designs upon the horse's legs.

Pig Bush marks no camp or village ; it is just a place-name and lies at the end of Tantany Wood. When we got there we saw the track I had marked as ours running off through the trees on our right. This track we were told by some lumbermen would, if we kept along by the enclosure fence, take us safely across the bog below Fernycroft Wood, over the Lyndhurst–Dibden road, and out on to Yew Tree Heath.

We followed their advice and went wrong, but we did not mind as the track was delightful and we were not led far out of our way. In fact it was rather a pleasant surprise when, after wandering along a path that went up and down and in and out among lovely old trees with woods and sometimes a paddock on one side, and the open heath on the other, we found ourselves back on the moor where we had seen our first shell-duck and recog-nised the lonely stone raised in memory of the sportsman's death.

Turning back we descended into a dip and saw at once the path we should have taken, running white and shining across the bog and up to Fernycroft. Our double journey along part of the track had discovered for me that not only were the trees sheltering it various and old, but they had their own ideas about mixed marriages and even polygamy. There were several unions of oak and beech, and once I saw two oaks and a beech springing up from the same root.

We crossed the bog, a narrow and not too interesting strip of coarse grasses and general sponginess, and climbed up the heathered slope to the pretty little oak and beech wood called Fernycroft.

The trees spread a good way beyond the railings, and under these freemen the track wanders. On our right were shadowed glades with buttercups in their damp hollows and foxgloves' purple distaffs standing above the young green bracken. On our left in the hollow below lay the jewel of the bog—a long, blue pool as still as sleep, with tiny pines and white cotton tufts at its margins and tussocks rising out of its depths. On one of these tussocks rested a shell-duck; at the opposite end of the pool stood a heron.

There was no wind to stir the branches above us or ruffle the water's surface, there were no clouds to give movement to the sky, neither of the birds below us so much as blinked an eye as far as we could see. Even the strong sunlight seemed to be tranced. The stillness was hypnotic; the dogs came to a stand at my side, staring unseeingly at the pool; and for myself, I felt as though I was rooted to the ground and had no will to stir.

Suddenly a horn sounded clear and sharp from the hidden road ahead, Bill swept down to the cool water like an arrow, the shell-duck whistled away over the encircling slopes, and the heron rose solemnly into the air and began to fly half-heartedly away. But the spell of the pool was too strong for him and, in spite of Bill's presence at the far end of it, he circled, and after hovering uncertainly above one of the little pine trees close to its edge, dropped deftly on to the topmost branches. Now he lost all his dignity, for the branches were little better than twigs and bent and swayed under his weight, making him tip back and forth, flap his half-spread wings, and treadle anxiously with his awkward legs. At last he got his balance and then stood up straight as a soldier and looking for all the world like a caricature of the glittering fairy doll on top of a Christmas tree.

At the end of the wood we crossed a gravel drive leading to the house concealed in Fernycroft, and taking the leftward of the two tracks meeting near it were soon across the Lyndhurst–Dibden road and on to Yew Tree Heath.

The views from the top of the heath of mile on mile of wild and wooded country are splendid. The heath itself is a fine, purple, undulating waste scarred here and there with white gravel diggings.

The track we followed went quickly and easily down its flank and brought us into a delightful little wooded bottom where the Beaulieu river drifted from one green arbour to another over shallow fords among grass and heather.

Where we crossed it the river had divided into one or two streams each with its small bridge and each filled with snowy water crowfoot, forget-me-nots, and butter-cups. In the deeper pools near the trees fawn-coloured cows stood in the shadows, dappled with sunlight on top, and underneath covered with the wriggling gold snakes of its reflection on the bright water. All round were the green-brown, purple streaked moorland hills shutting out the rest of the world and sheltering the lovely little valley from the world and rough weather.

Beyond the valley the path goes up and down, skirting boggy patches and climbing gently all the time. We surprised a curlew in a bit of dried bog, who by her behaviour must have had either young or eggs hidden hard by. Instead of rising high in the air and flying away, the poor bird acted with all the courage a plover shows in the same circumstances. She skimmed over the ground just in front of Bill, pitching occasionally when she got too far ahead and he began to lose interest in her—and all the time kept up a metallic, anxious chatter utterly unlike her usual lovely call. It was wonderful to watch her. Her courage was greater than the plover's because a plover is used to mankind and will hang about round his plough or harrow ready to deal with the grubs in the newly turned soil. But everyone knows that the curlew is afraid of us and our works, keeping as far as she can from us and making her home in the loneliest places she can find. Yet this bird not only came close enough for me to note her rich markings and the gleam on her long, curved bill, but sometimes actually ran along the ground towards me when I had got Bill to come to heel, hoping that she might induce the two of us to attack her instead of trying to find her nest.

I longed to be able to set her heart at rest by telling her that nothing would induce me to look for the nest as it worried her so, but as this could not be done I did the next best thing, which was to hurry up the track and over the ridge above the bog as fast as possible.

Below, across the falling moor, I saw some cottages, pine trees, and fields and knew that one of them was probably the Fox Hill Farm on our map and that therefore we should soon be in Long Down.

No one was at home in any of the cottages so we set off along a track running uphill on the left and before very long came upon the straggling hamlet of Long Down. It is an unattractive place but it lies fortunately. There are woods on three sides of it, the moor in front, and it is high up and looks across some of the boldest country in the Forest.

Not far out of the village we took on our left a track running over a green space dotted with trees and by it were brought to the gate of Deerleap Enclosure. At first the cool ride went levelly between tall pines and then shot down into a damp green hollow, from which it climbed steeply and at once. In this dip Bill suddenly stopped dead, then, head in air, zig-zagged a moment, uncertainly sniffling furiously the while ; then he went cracking away into the undergrowth.

For a few minutes there was no sound or movement other than those of his eager hunting, and then swift and sudden one silvery body after another leapt silently and smoothly across the grass ride. Hot on the deers' heels came a Bill it was no use to call, so Mr. Bundy and I reached the ride's top by ourselves and there awaited his return.

The ride was ended by another cutting straight across

At Beaulieu

it, and when Bill rejoined us we went down the new track right-handed and through a gate into Church Place Enclosure.

Church Place has about it the air of a deserted garden. Its rides are mostly so overgrown that one has to push through bushes to keep to them, but it is full of sun, charming young trees, and fine old ones. At last we got to a sound, well-kept track and, turning left, went downhill out of the trees, over a clearing and through a gate. A broad drive runs between Church Place and Ashurst Wood and up this we turned right-handed, went through another gate, and over a railway bridge on our left.

On the other side of the bridge under the oak trees fringing Ashurst Wood is a big brown pool filled with golden waterlilies.

From the pond to Lyndhurst no part of the way is without beauty. We followed the track through the trees until it left us at Ashurst Lodge and then took the gravel road which runs downhill under trees, crosses a bit of heath, and joins the Southampton highway near Ashurst station.

A track crossing the heath on the left led us through the enchanting outskirts of Mallard Wood, down into a wide heather bottom criss-crossed by waterways each bestrode by a bridge and bright with waterflowers, and then, skirting more trees, brought us to the foot of Bolton's Bench and the beginning of Lyndhurst.

By now we had covered about eight miles, and as nearly five miles more lay between us and Pig Bush I hailed an ice-cream barrow, bought three chilly packages, and then climbing to the top of the Bench, sat down and dealt them out.

It is a good place from which to look at the southern woods and plains, and it is peppered with rabbit holes. The rabbits are the most brazen I have ever seen. In spite of our nearness they sat with their head and shoulders above ground looking at anything but us, their ears transparent and pink in the sun, their funny noses twitching unceasingly. Strange to relate neither of the dogs showed the least interest in them, and I can only suppose that the ice-creams had frozen their sporting instincts.

Rested and refreshed we followed a broad sandy gallop running over the moors close to and parallel with the Beaulieu road. It began very soon to run downhill and when it got near to the oakwood called Matley we left it, crossing the road and entering another track. This we had to leave again nearly as soon as we entered it, for it took us back into the road by the bridge over Matley Bog. This is a pretty crossing, the swaying green alders closing up on either side of the bridge and trailing their leaves in the clear water of the bog-bred stream.

The road mounts up from the bridge, and where it curves away to the left we saw on the right the gravel track we wanted. The track looks as if it only leads to a gravel pit, but when we got to the pit we saw unfolding before us a glorious beech and oak avenue broken every now and then by patches of heath. On our left were the moors of Denny Walk, on the right was Denny Wood. The marges of the track were freshly green and still had a lot of bluebells growing on them, the branches were alive with birds all as noisily happy as they could be, and on the air was the scent of may and bluebells. Through this enchanting country we followed the road round curves, into dips, and up rises all the way to Denny Lodge and then entered the green track on the left by which some weeks back we had left Denny Bog.

Under a clear sky and bright sun the bog looked really cheerful; splendid dragonflies hovered and darted over its pools and the bogmyrtle had turned green and sweet smelling. On the other side we kept close to the rails of Denny Lodge Enclosure and walked along under firs and blossom-laden may trees until we came to an open, heathy rise. There we turned into the enclosure and a hundred yards or so up the wide ride took the first track we came to on the left. It was green, cool, and wet, the branches of the young trees stretched across it and hung down almost to the ground, the long grass was still covered with dew and hardly touched by the sun. A path mounting up on the right took us among the beeches of Woodfidley, where we lost it under the welter of cast leaves. The trees, we thought, were a little disappointing after the giants of Mark Ash and the ancients of Ridley and Anses.

Steering in the direction of the railway we came at length on a ride, up which we turned right and followed it until we came to a pretty path running bumpily and steeply down into one we already knew. It was the track by which we came from Brockenhurst to Bishops Dike, and to-day it was a-quiver with dragonflies. They were splendid fellows, with slim glittering green and gold

227

bodies, mighty opal eyes, and wings that whizzed so fast it looked as if each insect hung in its own little patch of mist. There were so many of them one could almost imagine the humming drone of the aeroplane, hidden from us by the trees, was coming from their wings.

Outside on the edge of Bishops Dike we went right and over the railway bridge, which is lucky in having ponds and trees at its side and from which are grand views of the moors.

We now had before us a pleasant, well-marked track which kept under the trees near Frame Heath Enclosure's railings, and when we reached the gate we turned away from the woods and bore with it to the left.

Now it took us over gently rising and falling ground, through delicious little oakwoods and across open, springy-turfed patches. When it ended we turned left down a way so faintly marked that we practically felt our way along it, but which brought us safely to the edge of the bog. Here it turned strong-minded and quickly led on to the low bridge over the stream which drains the bog. We were now at Pig Bush passage and, when we saw the fine gravel track coming to the bridge from over the moors and running up to the trees of Pig Bush on the other side, realised that we had come to it by rather a roundabout route. But the way had been too pleasant for regrets and when we come this way again it will still be our choice.

CHAPTER XIII

ROADS AND VILLAGES

To those who like road walking the Forest has as much to offer as it has to the lover of quiet woodland path and lonely moorland track. It is safe to say that there are no ugly or uninteresting roads in all this part of Hampshire and many that are really inspiring. Even the great tarmac highways become things of beauty as soon as they enter the Forest. Take, for instance, the main road from Southampton to Bournemouth.

What could be more soul-destroying—except the latter part of its journey—than its first four miles out of Southampton? First Millbrook, once so pretty, with its sad, vacant-eyed old houses from whose walls the plaster peels like bark from a plane tree, its old church where no one worships now standing dreary and broken-windowed by the noisy roadside, its garages and ugly rows of little buildings not worthy of the lovely name of cottages, and the cranes and concrete, smoke and iron of the world's biggest dock a-building on the water's edge. Then like a ray of hope come the bridges over the river, one old and built of grey stone, the others mighty bows of modern concrete ; here are splendid reed-beds, deep channels, a clump of elm trees, a few brightly painted boats and several pretty old buildings. But over the bridges is —— Totton. And the worst of Totton is that you cannot race through and get it over quickly, because there is a speed limit. After Totton comes Hounsdown, where things begin to get better, for there are two or three old thatched cottages with proper country gardens, and a chestnut tree that holds its branches out across the road like a blessing.

230

Next comes a tree-crowned hill, which is only right, for it is the gateway into the Forest.

Though red brick and petrol pump punctuate the green descent to Ashurst the road improves in appearance at once, for it is graced with grass verges, hedges, and trees. Beyond the station it puts on the beauty which never drops away until it quits the Forest boundary on Plain Heath.

Nearly all the way to Lyndhurst woods line its two sides. It slips into the town across an open space, switchbacks out of it under more trees, sweeps across a wide furzy grazing ground and then winds, dips, and climbs through the great woods of Knightwood, Vinney, Dames Slough, Rhinefield Sandys, and Burley New, crossing four little rivers on the way; then it mounts up Markway Hill across the moors, drops down beside Wilverly Enclosure, goes over the Avon Water-cum-railway bridge above Holmsley station, and uphill again past Holmsley, on to Plain Heath. From there on it gradually becomes more and more sophisticated until it gets to Christchurch, and after Christchurch it becomes past all hope for the rest of the way to Bournemouth.

For road walks in the north we think Fritham is still the best centre—unless the walker requires an hotel. In that case we substitute Stoney Cross.

People who like road walking are, we have noticed, inclined to sniff pityingly at a mere ten miles or so, therefore we have mapped out a few routes averaging about twenty miles. Our knowledge, such as it is, of these tarmac and gravel ways is not born of shoe leather and pad, but of

Miss Riley's tyres. Our acquaintance with them, therefore, is of the passing kind.

I

This is a grand route. Start from Fritham, go round by Ironswell on to the highway, turn left and follow it straight across the moors to Godshill. Go down the winding, wooded hill which comes to the Avon's edge and, bearing right, cross the river by Fordingbridge's old stone bridge, for the little town is well worth seeing. It has ancient charm still in spite of enamel signs and orange tea-umbrellas, it lies in water-meadows and is surrounded by wooded hills. The church has a lime walk and in the Lady Chapel is a marvellous fifteenth-century timber roof all angels and tracery. In the old days the lord of the manor had to maintain an armed guard on the bridge during the fifteen days before and after Midsummer Day to deal with deer stealers.

Take the Ringwood highway and keep to it until a lane bears off to the right. At first it goes through hedges but soon exchanges them for the river bank and lovely views of water-meadows and elms and wooded hills. It goes straight as a die to Bickton, a village beloved by painters. Here is a big water-mill with weirs, noisy race, and a big still pool where wild swan and mallard float and dabble peacefully with the prosaic quackers of the village.

An old lady who used to live at Bickton told me that nearly every cottage had its ducks and that in the evening it was an amusing pastime for the villagers to watch the birds leave the water in a body, proceed along the lane, and as the different cottages were reached break up into separate companies each bound for its own particular gate.

The cottages have thatched porches and pretty gardens, and at the far end of the village is a beautiful old farm-house whose green lawns drop sharply down to the river.

The lane goes through Bickton and curves back to the highway and crosses it into the Gorley or Moyles Court road. Take the right fork (the left goes up to Hyde and Hampton Ridge) and go through the Gorleys to Moyles Court. Cross the stream and, turning left, go up the Linwood road, which, climbing all the time, winds along the foot of Rockford Common, passes Appleslade and Roe Wood, and then drives across Broomy and Ocknell Plains to Jane's Moor and Fritham.

Here are some variations. *The first variation* adds seven or eight miles to the route. At Telegraph Hill go right instead of to Godshill and follow the road out of the Forest and out of Hampshire as well. Something under half a mile from North Charford take a road on the left; it brings you into Downton.

At Downton are a beautiful old market cross, an inn with what are said to be thirteenth-century wooden busts of King John and Queen Isabella in niches in its front, an ancient church. and a famous earthwork called the Moot. There is thirteenth, fourteenth, and fifteenth-century work in the church, which is built of iron-stone and quite impressive. The font is Norman, and in a memorial window are some lovely pieces of old glass.

The Moot is said to have begun life as a British-built

233

fortress, but the Saxons made tiers of earthen seats all round its inside and turned it into a meeting place.

Leave Downton by the road passing the Moot and follow it for two and a half miles past watermeadows to Woodgreen, on through Godshill Enclosure, down into Millersford Bottom and up on to the highway by the ' Fighting Cocks.'

Another variation. At the top of the hill instead of descending to Fordingbridge take a turning on the left. This lane turns and twists uphill and down, goes through Blissford and Frogham, crosses Hyde Common, and drops into the Gorley road through Frogham.

A third variation. At the bottom of the hill instead of going right-handed into Fordingbridge turn left and go along the pretty road which ambles through Stuckton to the Gorleys.

II

Go over Longcross Plain, down Bramble Hill to No Man's Land, follow the boundary road through Bramshaw to Cadnam, and opposite the low whitewashed thatched inn, standing near the cross-roads, turn up the Ringwood highway and keep to it for nine glorious miles.

Up through the woods of Castle Malwood it goes, then swings up and down across the moors for about six miles without passing a single building from Stoney Cross to Picket Post, or touching cover except for the wooded steep of Bratley.

A mile below Picket Post take the second turning on the right and follow it down into Poulner (pronounced

Powner should you have to ask for it) and when the road
ends go right again. The new road goes straight for a
while, then does a quick left and right between a pretty
little farm and a stagnant pool, and crosses the Linbrook
at a pretty splash with a pollard oak leaning over it, a
gorse-covered little green and a white footbridge. Fields
and wooded hills lie round it. Bear left at the ford and
then keep straight on to Moyles Court. Do not cross the
ford there but go up the Linwood road and so back to
Fritham.

III

This is a ' quick one.'

Take the Jane's Moor road, cross the highway at Stoney
Cross, and then about a mile and a quarter farther on take
the turning on the left to Minstead.

Minstead's claims to fame are a three-decker pulpit, a
manorial pew with a fireplace and easy chairs, and an inn
sporting the ' Faithful Servant ' sign. The church stands
by itself on a hillock under trees, has dormer windows,
low galleries, and a fine old font. In the graveyard I found
at the back of the church a headstone on which was
carved that wondrous and weird wind instrument called
the serpent. The musician asleep below was, if I remember rightly, in the band of the old Hampshire Volunteers.

From Minstead several lanes lead off to the Lyndhurst
highway. To make the walk as long as possible, that is
about fifteen miles, take the lane that goes to Furzy Lawn,
here turn left, and when you get to Cadnam follow the
Fordingbridge road back to Long Cross.

From Lyndhurst

Though Hudson loathed Lyndhurst, to such an extent that he avoided it like the plague, we can forgive it its dreadful church and horrid red brick because of the show that is held there every April.

At this show stallions of all ages compete for premiums, and it is here that the coveted Ashley Challenge Cup and Bramble Memorial Cup are awarded.

It is a thrilling show for those who love a good pony and delight to see him at his best. The handsome little beasts go proudly round the various rings, some dancing, rearing, and plunging, others behaving with the most courtly dignity. The air is shrill with their challenges; they squeal, they grunt, or they whicker quietly to a field companion. There is human laughter and happy shouting, too, and stern commands.

In one corner of the field the agistors are taking grazing fees from owners, and with clasp knives are cutting hanks of hair from their ponies' tails in receipt. Exciting battles are taking place down by the lorries parked under the trees. Groups of four or five men, laughing and shouting, are hauling, pushing, and slapping ponies they wish to embark. The ponies resort to all sorts of eel-like antics to avoid returning to the dark interior of the vans, but it is seldom that they ' land out ' and intentionally damage their attendants.

Of course these battles are not necessary, the older hands simply slip a second rope round the pony's haunches, place a man at each end of it, and when the man on

236

MR. BRAMBLE WITH MRS. GROSVENOR'S ORCHARD PERSHORE

THE SPORTING PIG

the halter rope gives the word and a hearty pull himself they fairly lift the animal into the lorry with no trouble at all. I have even seen it done with a stout cane instead of the breeching rope. But most of the men are out for ' a bit of sport,' and a tussle with a stout, spirited young pony in a hemp halter is just what they like.

Apart from the show people come to Lyndhurst to see the Verderers' Hall, where Forest affairs are still settled and Forest offences dealt with. I do not know whether deer stealing is punishable here, as legally there are no deer in the Forest. An Act ordering their removal was passed in the nineteenth century, and those that live in the Forest now have found their way here themselves and are the property of nobody in particular I suppose. It would be interesting to know quite what steps could be taken against a person convicted of killing a legally non-existent beast of venery.

In the Hall are the huge and ancient dock, some Tudor panelling, a pair of interlocked antlers belonging to two bucks found dead and thus entangled all for the love of a lady, and a large stirrup iron. This stirrup purports to be the one through which in old days a dog had to be able to pass if he wished to preserve his middle front claws. Mr. Bundy would have gone through the ordeal triumphantly, but it would have left poor Bill a cripple for life.

Lyndhurst is an excellent centre for road walking, or for our kind of walking, as it lies within reach of woods, moors, and sea-coast. If it were not so suburbanised we should have declared in its favour instead of voting in

Burley's, but its horrid brick, its garages and shops are more than we could stand.

I

Follow the tarmac Bournemouth highway until you get to the end of Knightwood Enclosure, then exchange it for the Burley Lodge road. At Burley ask for the Thorney Hill road, and when you have crossed the lovely moor and climbed up to Thorney Hill take the first turning on the right. The little road is quiet, and at first commands splendid views of the Avon valley and the country beyond. On one side is the deep heathered basin below Thorney Hill church, and on the other, lying at the foot of more heather-covered slopes, are the woods and lakes of Avon Tyrrell; ahead stretch the meadows, trees, and hills that line the Avon's banks all the way to Christchurch.

As the road descends, fields and spinneys begin; you pass through Shirley and Ripley and come out on the Christchurch road in the riverside village of Avon.

Avon Farm, the home of Mr. Bramble, is an important place, because it stands hard by the ford through which Walter Tyrrell rode when flying from the dead king in Canterton glen. You cannot mistake the farm, as it is on the bend of the road with an open green in front of it, and has a range of buildings round it so true to Tudor tradition that at first glance they have taken in more than one expert. As a matter of fact they were built in the nineteenth century. If you want to see the ford Mr. Bramble will give permission if you ask him.

238

From Avon Farm go north, that is, towards Ringwood, and then take the first turning on the right. Keep on through North Ripley, turn left at the cross-roads, go through Sandford, and just short of North Kingston take the road on the right. It will take you to the Crow road, where you must turn right again, go up Crow Hill, past Knaves Ash and into the Burley road. From Avon you will have had beside you spinneys, fields, and green fences, and will have passed through groups of pretty cottages not big enough to merit the name of village. At Knaves Ash the road runs between Vales Moor and Cranes Moor, fine stretches of heather country and bog with Burley's wooded hills lying ahead.

At the Burley road turn up it left, following it along the top of the moor to Picket Post. On the right you have the heather, Ridley Wood and the miles of plain and wood beyond ; on the left, country changing from moor to wood, from wood to pastureland, and far, far away the grand downs of Dorset.

At Picket Post is a cottage with a big gold kettle hanging out for a sign that within is meat and drink. Opposite is a well-grazed green and a pond where ponies and cattle are usually to be found.

Follow the highway across the moors, down under Bratley's lovely old beeches, and half-way up the hill take the turning to Lyndhurst. It goes along the top of Mogshade Hill, giving you gorgeous views of the Forest before burying itself under the trees and descending into Emery Down and Lyndhurst.

II

Go to Brockenhurst along the beautiful road running between woods all the way to Balmer Lawn. The old church here has a derelict oak of colossal age, and in the graveyard lies a famous Forest character, Brusher Mills, the man who spent his life catching adders for the zoo's hamadryads. He has a big marble headstone on which he is shown, carved in relief, against a background of his beloved Forest trees, with his victims and the paraphernalia he used in catching them carefully chiselled too.

I was told, or read, I forget which, a sorry story about this old man's death. He lived in a small hut such as charcoal burners use, and had occupied it nearly long enough to make its site his own property, according to a Forest custom which has it that should you stay undisturbed for a certain number of years in a hut on a piece of Forest ground that ground becomes your property. Brusher had only a day or so to go before he could claim his little house, and boasted about it too widely. One night he came home to find no hut, only a heap of smoking ashes. Shortly after this he was found dead in the snow outside one of the Forest inns.

Leaving Brockenhurst behind, cross Setley Plain and at Batramsley Cross take the Boldre road. Follow its delightful windings down to the stone bridge over the river, go up through Pilley Street past the school Gilpin founded for the children of his parish, and when you get to upland Pilley Bailey on the fringe of Beaulieu Heath

Sweetman

BEAULIEU ABBEY—REFECTORY AND CLOISTERS

turn right. Quarter of a mile farther on go left and keep along through Bulhill, Norley . Enclosure and Norley-wood (a village), and when the road ends turn left. When this road is met by another turn up the new road right, and then, bearing left with it all the time, follow it round past Sowley Pond and into the road to St. Leonards Grange. From St. Leonards make your way to Beufre and Beaulieu ; from Beaulieu go back to Lyndhurst across the moors and bogs.

III

Take the road across the moors to Beaulieu, and when you reach the bend above Matley bridge leave it for the gravel road which appears to be leading into the gravel pit. This runs through glorious woods all the way to Ladycross Lodge, passing Denny Lodge and Settlement on the way. At Ladycross Lodge it joins the Brocken-hurst-Beaulieu highway. Go through Beaulieu, keep on past the ruins and up the hill on to the Hill Top Heath. Here take the road to Exbury where there is a perfect little church, simple as honesty. The bronze figure of a youth who was killed in the world war reposes under the tower on a tomb with a tall bronze torch at each corner, and on the roll of honour are the lines :

> O valiant hearts who to your glory came
> Through dust of conflict and through battle flame,
> Tranquil you lie, your knightly virtue proved,
> Your memory hallowed by the land you loved.

One cannot see the big white house where William Mitford, the historian of Greece and friend of Edward

Gibbon, lived because it is hidden by its trees and rhododendrons.

A rough lane goes down to Lower Exbury, and idles
along to Lepe between fences which screen the Solent,
but we like to follow the road on its wandering journey
between fields, under trees, and past farmhouses because
it springs Lepe and the Solent on us as a surprise.
Bathers, motor-cars, and ice-cream barrows are all to be
seen at Lepe, but as yet there are only a very few houses.

Turning inland the road goes along the Forest border
to Langley, and passing the road to Fawley leaves the
Forest above Buttsash and joins the Beaulieu-Hythe road.
Hythe appeals to some but leaves us cold in spite of its
view of the docks ; there are so many irritating houses and
its church is very nineteenth century. So at this point
we take the turning to Dibden, about quarter of a mile
up the highway towards Beaulieu, and, when we have
looked at the docks and liners across the Water from the
graveyard of the tiny church, take the road to Long Down
and follow it to Colbury and the Lyndhurst highway.

Neither Fawley nor Dibden are in the Forest, but both
have churches overhanging Southampton Water. Fawley
church has, among other attractions, a handsomely carved
Norman doorway and other striking Norman sculpture
on the capitals of several pillars. It also possesses one of
the oldest pieces of church plate in England, a little silver-
gilt paten believed to have been William of Wickham's
gift. In Dibden's church the altar rails are said to
have been made from a great yew tree once standing in
the graveyard.

IV

From Emery Down keep on to Stoney Cross, over Jane's Moor into Fritham, down through the noble woods along Hampton Ridge to Frogham. Take the Moyles Court road, turn up to Linwood and go under the trees to Roe Cottage. Follow the road through Roe Wood over the moor, across the Ringwood highway into the track through Bratley Wood, up past Boldrewood Farm on to Boldrewood Green. Take the track through the woods, and when you reach the Lyndhurst highway either turn up it to Lyndhurst or cross it into Vinney Ridge and go back to Lyndhurst from Brockenhurst.

CHAPTER XIV

MORE INTERESTING VIL LAGES AND A HOTEL OR TWO

THOUGH there are only a very few interesting villages in the Forest itself, the borders are studded with them. Along the road which follows the Avon from Salisbury to Christchurch stand Downton, Charford, Breamore, Fordingbridge, Ellingham, Ringwood, Avon, Sopley, and Burton, all pretty, all interesting, and all easy to find.

We have already said what we know about Downton and so will start with Charford. It is a scattered parish, whose claim to fame is the beautiful water-meadows lying between the Salisbury and the Hale roads. They are enchanting now with their countless streams, tiny weirs and bridges, their long grasses and pollard willows, but once they were a stretch of treacherous marshes deep in rank reeds. It is practically certain that it was in these marshes ' Ambrosius Aurelianus, Prince Natan-Leod, father of the great Arthur of mediaeval legends ' made his last stand against and suffered his last defeat at the all-conquering hands of Cerdic the Saxon. He and five thousand of his warriors were killed on the Avon's edge (the river ran through the marsh), but Wise, from whom we got our information, does not say whether the prince was given burial or whether the victors left him where he fell. We rather hope they left him, because it is tremendous to think that here in this green valley King Arthur's sire lies.

Breamore is close to Charford and has hidden behind its roadside cottages a rising green with a little brook running down it, a few trees, and geese and cattle to graze it smooth. In a nearby field are the remains of an

246

ancient Austin priory, and on the edge of the manor house's park is the small church, famous because so much of it is early Saxon. Round the tower's southern arch is an inscription in Saxon characters six inches high meaning, ' Here the Covenant becomes manifest to thee,' and on the wall of what was once the porch's upper room is a big rood. The main group is very much damaged but the landscape behind the cross is quite clear.

The Elizabethan manor house was nearly completely destroyed by fire in the late nineteenth century, but I believe I am right in saying that one wing was saved. The rebuilding was most successful, as we have seen for ourselves on our few expeditions to the downs above. It is a beautiful walk to take up to the downs, even when accompanied by dogs whose longing to plunge into the game-filled undergrowth of the woods, through which the path rises at first, make leads a necessity. Free of the woods you come out on the downs and follow a line of dark yews to a big tree-covered mound, on whose top is a clearing. In the centre of the clearing is the Miz-Maz, the second of Breamore's claims to distinction. Beyond the fact that it is of immense age, no one knows anything about the Miz-Maz. Some say it was probably the work of the Austin priors, and some that it was made long before their time. It is circular and most intricate though not very large. The downs are rich in flowers, viper's bugloss especially flourishing there, and from the top one can look across miles of noble, though cultivated, country.

Lying back between Breamore and Fordingbridge, reached by lanes so narrow, winding, rough, and wooded

that a car looks quite uncomfortable among them, is
Rockbourne. It is so engaging a little place that we
would find our way to it were the lanes twice as confusing
as they are. The stream which christens it flows right
through it, so that the cottages on its far side have had to
hook themselves to the road by means of small bridges.
The church, which is filled with the monuments of the
Eyre Cootes and has a Norman doorway and early
English arcade, stands on a steep knoll above an old farmhouse and some splendid stone barns. In the time of the
Stuarts this was the manor house of the father of
Dryden's ' false Achitophel,' that Lord Shaftesbury of
whom Charles II said that he was the wickedest fellow
in the dominions. It is said that ' Achitophel ' replied
respectfully, ' Of a subject, Sire, I believe I am.'

The Eyre Cootes lived in West Park, the big house near
the village. In the park is a pillar commemorating the
capture of Pondicherry in 1761 by Sir Eyre Coote. His
monument in the church is the humblest of all—if I
remember rightly—and, I think, is tucked away by the
pulpit.

Ringwood's charm comes from the Avon, the lovely
water-meadows through which it wanders in two wide
clear streams, and the lime-bordered causeway and
bridges which cross them. In the cold months we have
stood by the red brick power station, on the railed-in
concrete bank, watching the salmon leaping up the roaring
weir, while in the shallows the dorsal fins of those resting,
after several unsuccessful attempts, showed moving
smoothly and lazily about.

Apart from an eighteenth-century chapel (kept locked, unfortunately) with high box pews, a charming old lacquer clock, and a painted plaster-work ceiling, there is only one building of any interest in Ringwood. It is the shabby little white house near some pretty thatched and timbered cottages, standing on the Avon's edge near the first bridge. Ringwood says, and firmly believes, that it was to this house that Monmouth was brought after his capture on the Dorset border, and that under this roof he wrote his pitiful appeals for mercy to James II. Unhappily the old church was pulled down, but the new one is worth seeing because of the handsome way in which the organ has been built in; this has been so cleverly and intelligently done that it has given the whole church a beauty and dignity it never had before. Under a mat beside the choir-stalls is the very fine brass of John Prophete, at one time Ringwood's rector and later on Dean of Hereford and York. He died in 1416.

Of all the next villages, Bill considers the most important to be Avon, and I too regard it with the most affection. Not only is it lovely with great elms, green fields, the glittering, curving Avon, and the distant pine-covered ridge above Hurn, but it is where we come to spend exciting, happy days with Mr. and Mrs. Bramble. Grand days walking very quietly over the furrows with eager greyhounds held in leash until away down a furrow a crouching form is picked out, when the hounds are slipped, but only at the last minute. Puss always wins, and that's what makes it so joyous to watch her sunlit, brown body racing and doubling and dodging, and the strong lithe greyhounds straining every nerve to come up with her. Fine days too when the rickyard is filled with the throbbing hum of the threshing machine, and as the rick gets low great brown rats make bold bids for freedom, which seldom succeed because Bill is there expressly to see that they should not, and because the men are marvellously dexterous with boot and stick in dealing with the rats that bolt where Bill doesn't happen to be. It was in this yard I learned that hens are first-rate mousers ! Mice in hundreds escape through the wire netting surrounding the rick, and once the rats begin to appear Bill will not stop for a mouse. It is then that the hens may be seen tearing along after little bounding grey bodies or wandering about with tiny, mangled corpses dangling from their beaks. *Before* the rats come to the surface Bill shows a quite too awful interest in mice ; in fact there is a horrible and absolutely bona-fide story of his actually eating thirty-six of the poor little wretches in one afternoon !

On the roadside, at the beginning of a lane a little above Avon Farm, is a low, square stone building which people like to think was the forge where Tyrel had his horse shod backwards so that his pursuers would be misled as to the direction in which he was going.

Sopley is a lovely village and has a perfect little church standing on a green bluff overlooking an old mill and the Avon. It has a low tower and tiny spire and was built mostly in the thirteenth and fifteenth centuries. Over the porch is an excellent stone figure of St. Michael and inside the church are two good, though mutilated, corbel heads of Edward III and his queen. The arcades are simple and lofty and the oak roof is carried by corbels on which are carved angels playing the viol and double pipe. The pulpit and a big carved chair in the chancel are both early seventeenth century; on the chair back is carved a coat-of-arms with a man holding a sheaf of wheat as a crest. For those interested in such things there is a low side window with a shutter to close it. The east window's top lights are filled with ancient heraldic glass—angels holding shields, a lion's head, and a flaming brazier; lovely stuff whose rich, mellow colours shame the gaudy glass below. On either side of the door are two Purbeck marble canopied gravestones with the mutilated figures of the founder and his wife upon them. The man has a simple civilian dress and his lady a high-collared, pleated cloak and a beaded wimple.

Through Winkton, where the Avon comes right up to the roadside, you come to Burton. Burton is pretty too, like all the Avon's villages. It has trees, a handsome old house in a walled garden, a green, and a long low white-washed thatched cottage which once belonged to Southey. When Southey came there were two cottages, but he turned them into one and wrote ecstatic letters to his friends about his new home, its garden, and its view over the water-meadows to Christchurch and St. Catherine's Hill. Among those of his friends who stayed here with him was Charles Lamb, who came in the summer of 1797. Lamb did not succumb to Burton's charm, however, being homesick for London.

Two miles on is Christchurch, still a lovely old town in spite of its *nouveau riche* neighbours. It is under a

251

cloud from our point of view though, because the authorities practise the unholy custom of charging the would-be visitor to the minster an entrance fee. We feel that Christians should at least be free to enter their church and so content ourselves with the minster's external beauties.

Mudeford, just to the east of Christchurch, though afflicted with 'bungaloid growth,' has three great redeeming features. It is on the sea, and across shingle and sandbanks, a strongly running tidal river, and a sea usually of a vivid peacock blue looks at the Isle of Wight, the Needles and their lighthouse. The second feature is the house standing among ilex and tamarisk on top of a stone ramp rising straight out of the beach. It was built by Sir Walter Scott's friend, Stewart Rose, himself a bit of a poet, and is called Gundimore. Both Scott and Coleridge stayed here, and their visits were recorded by their host in his poem ' Gundimore.'

> Here Walter Scott has wooed the Northern Muse,
> Here he with me has joyed to walk or cruize ;
> And hence has pricked through Ytene's holt, where we
> Have called to mind how under greenwood tree,
> Pierced by the partner of his ' woodland craft,'
> King Rufus fell by Tiril's random shaft.
> Hence have we ranged by Keltic camps and barrows,
> Or climbed the expectant bark, to thread the Narrows
> Of Hurst, bound westward to the gloomy bower
> Where Charles was prisoned in yon island tower.
>
>   *   *   *   *   *   *   *
>
> Here, witched from summer sea and softer reign,
> Foscolo courted Muse of milder strain.

252

On these ribbed sands was Coleridge pleased to pace
Whilst ebbing seas have hummed a rolling base
To his rapt talk.

Walter Scott wrote part of *Marmion* at Gundimore.

The third feature is Hengistbury Head, the great whale-like headland which is the southward defence of Christchurch Harbour. The harbour is formed by the rivers Avon and Stour, which meet below Christchurch and spread out into a wide lake before the sandbanks of Mudeford force them into one stream. They join the sea about half-way to Highcliffe—an unnatural sort of place, as its added 'e' suggests.

To reach Hengistbury from Mudeford one follows the sandy, fir-lined track along the harbour's edge to Black House. Black House, a handful of fishermen's tarred cottages, was once a meeting place for the smugglers; now, for most people, it merely means the place where they get the ferry to Hengistbury. A fisherman charges a few pence to row one across in a boat which seems perilously low in the water. For about half a mile or under one then walks over cream-coloured sandbanks tufted with coarse grass and festooned with drying nets, and along a beach where the waves come rolling sideways on to the hard sand at a speed that explains why bathing is discouraged here; then one comes up to the stoutly rising side of the headland. The path winds through gorse and low little bushes up on to the bare heather-covered top, where the wind gives one a buffet of welcome and the view across the sea is unbounded.

Mr. Sumner says, ' The excavations (1911–12) at

Hengistbury Head—formerly within the New Forest boundary—show that this harbour settlement was occupied throughout the Iron Age. Metal-working, spinning, and weaving were carried on here ; cereals were cultivated, and grain was ground in stone querns. . . . This site is classic, inasmuch as here British Iron Age pottery was first identified. . . .'

A road runs along the coast from Christchurch to Lymington, but on this stretch, apart from Mudeford, there are, we report sadly, only two villages where there is anything worth stopping for. Old Milton, badly mauled by modern builder and architect, keeps under the tower of its church an attractive eighteenth-century monument. Under a canopy festooned with fruit and flowers, and draped with gilded curtains held apart by cherubs, is the armoured effigy of Thomas White, a bewigged and portly gentleman in armour holding a short, wavy-bladed sword in one hand and his helmet in the other. His real sword, a lovely thing with delicately carved hilt and wavy blade, is padlocked to the monument. His epitaph says he was much wounded in the Irish and Flemish wars and that he served under three kings and Queen Anne. The tower itself is old but the rest of the church, fortunate in its oak chancel screen and choir-stalls and its stone floor, is modern.

The road between Old Milton and Milford keeps the sea and the Island in sight nearly all the time ; it passes close to the neglected graveyard of Hordle's old church, of which only the Saxon foundations remain. In Milford one has the pleasure of finding some nice old houses still standing among the scarlet and roughcast riff-raff that is springing up with alarming speed on this coast, and a large, old church. Its low thirteenth-century tower has a string course of little faces round the top and a lead spire said to be fourteenth century. There is a good deal of Norman and thirteenth-century work in the building— one plate traceried thirteenth-century window particularly is pointed to with pride, and also a perfectly lovely little thirteenth-century doorway. On a wall is fixed a defaced but still graceful carving of the Annunciation, part of the old stone reredos which was found buried under the floor.

Personally I love to linger at Lymington as long as my companions will allow. So many of its charming old houses belong to the days when it was an important port and a fashionable health resort. In St. Thomas Street one of these houses is still known as ' Quadrille Court,' a name it got because the officers of the Hessian Corps, which had its headquarters here in 1756, used to meet there to play the then popular game. Of Lymington's other charms we have spoken already, and so will just mention that one can stay at the ' Angel ' or ' Londesborough ' hotels quite reasonably. The first charges 6s. for a single room, the other from 4s. to 8s. a single room.

From Lymington one can either follow the road down past Buckland Rings and across Setley Plain to Brockenhurst, or, crossing the river by the bridge Captain Cross built in 1731, follow the winding, enchanting coastal lanes past Sowley Pond to Buckler's Hard and Beaulieu. Or, again, if the left turning across the bridge is taken,

255

gain Beaulieu Heath and at Hatchet Pond choose between Brockenhurst and Beaulieu. At Beaulieu, by the way, is the 'Montagu Arms,' a hotel which charges from 8s. 6d. a room.

The right-hand road of the three meeting near the inn at Beaulieu Hilltop Heath goes through Exbury and Lepe, lonely no longer except in winter because the town-cramped motorist has discovered its humble shores and grand views, and then goes on to put one in the way of Calshot, Fawley, Dibden, and Eling.

Calshot has one of the stubby fortresses King Henry VIII built along the coast, using the stone from the ravished abbeys to do so, but it is so surrounded by the paraphernalia of the R.A.F. that it can only be seen to advantage from the water. Of course one can get permission to visit it, or so I understand.

Near Fawley, and reached by a little lane, is Ashlett creek, a delightful corner on the Water, with a quay and an ancient mill. Of Fawley and Dibden and Hythe we spoke in the last chapter and so will go straight on to Eling.

It stands at the head of Southampton Water, facing Millbrook across that broad stream. It has a quay, an old inn called the 'Anchor' which they will tell you was there five hundred years ago, a church whose Saxon arch is one of the many proofs that the Conqueror did not destroy all the churches in the New Forest so that the deer should not be incommoded by them, and a lovely old rectory whose lawn slopes down to the Water's edge and whose trees tower mightily about it.

256

HENGISTBURY HEAD, NEAR CHRISTCHURCH

In the centre of the rectory's garden is a great monument to a dog whose master used to live here generations ago. The two used to go swimming together and one day the master got into difficulties, whereupon the dog seized him by his long hair and towed him safely to shore.

There are many things I like to remember about Eling church. First there are its bells, ancient fellows recast in 1775, and five of them inscribed. One says,

> ' Ye ringers all that prize
> Your health and happiness
> Be sober, merry, wise
> And you'll the same possess,'

and the others,

> 'Peace and good neighbourhood,'

> 'Ye people that do hear me ring,
> Be faithful to your God and King,'

> 'I mean to make it understood,
> Though I am little I am good,'

and the last,

> ' Altho' I am both light and small,
> I will be heard above you all.'

The two last might apply to Mr. Bundy.

Then there is the beautiful brass candelabra with a dove carrying an olive branch in its beak. This three hundred year old masterpiece was found by the present rector thrown on the scrap heap at one of his earlier livings. Enquiring about it he was told it was waiting there until the tinker came by when it would be sold for about 15s. The rector bought it and took it with him when he left.

A gilded helmet with a flaming castle for crest hangs in the north aisle near the Saxon arch. The chancel arch is Early English, and over the altar is a fine altar piece painted by Marziale, the sixteenth-century Venetian artist. Eling owes this painting to Mr. Thistle as well as the candelabra, for it was he who discovered it rolled up in the tower and had it brought to light and reinstated.

In the graveyard are two headstones with quaint epitaphs. One runs,

> ' This world's a farce and all things show it
> I thought so once and now I know it.'

The other is on the grave of William Mansbridge of Cadnam,

> ' Stop reader pray and read my fate
> What caused my life to terminate.
> For thieves by night when in my bed
> Broak up my house and shot me dead.'

Writing of epitaphs reminds me of two others. The first I saw for myself in a Wiltshire church porch, the second was told to me by a friend who cannot remember where she saw it.

The Wiltshire one says, ' Received of Philip Herd, his borrowed earth July 4th, 1673 '; the other was on the grave of a poor old pauper woman and ran,

> ' Poorly lived, poorly died,
> Poorly buried, and nobody cried.'

Eling possesses some of the finest church plate in the county. It was made in 1693, is of solid silver, gilded and decorated with acanthus leaves, and consists of a chalice, paten-cover, paten, and a flagon which holds seven pints.

My memory is so bad that I cannot be sure if I am speaking the truth in saying that at Eling there are some meadows named Coblands, after the forester who owned them in Rufus' time and who supplied the King and his court with the arrows they used when hunting in the New Forest. With all diffidence I further set down that it was one of Cob's arrows which killed the king.

What I do know for certain is that Richard Lord Cromwell came to Eling to officiate at the wedding of a Thomas Burgess and Elizabeth Russell, for it is in the registers.

On the northern borders of the Forest are Cadnam, Bramshaw, and Brook. A few miles out towards Romsey lie the Wellows East and West, where Florence Nightingale lived and where she is buried. Apart from her grave people visit Wellow church because of its ancient charms, such as the thirteenth-century wall paintings of flowers, saints and kings, the aged nail-studded door, and the fourteenth-century low-side window.

Of Cadnam little can be said other than that it has beautiful woods immediately in front of it, a handsome topiary ship in a roadside garden, and two inns, one picturesque with thatch and plaster, the other interesting because it is mentioned in the following extract from Gilpin's *Remarks on Forest Scenery*, which is quoted from Mr. Sumner's *Guide to the New Forest*. The extract deals with an oak which once stood at Cadnam and was said to break into leaf in December.

259

'Having often heard of this oak, I took a ride to see it on the 29th day of December, 1781. It was pointed out to me among several other oaks, surrounded by a little Forest stream, winding round a knoll, on which they stood. It is a tall, straight plant of no great age and apparently vigorous ; except that its top had been injured ; from which several branches issue in the form of pollard shoots. It was entirely bare of leaves, as far as I could discern, when I saw it ; and undistinguishable from the other oaks in its neighbourhood ; except that its bark seemed rather smoother, occasioned I apprehended, only by frequent climbing. Having had the account of its early budding confirmed on the spot, I engaged one Michael Lawrence, who kept the White Hart, a small ale-house in the neighbourhood, to send me some leaves to Vicar's Hill, as soon as they should appear. The man who had not the least doubt about the matter, kept his word ; and sent me several twigs on the morning of the 5th January, 1782 ; a few hours after they had been gathered. . . .'

Mr. Sumner says, ' Two points may be noted in this account. (1) It mentions that the tree had been injured. (2) Twigs, with leaves on them, are assumed to represent similar vegetation all over the tree. A ' super-annivated ' Cadnam woodman tells me that the only evidence of such traditional growth is to be found in premature shoots around tree injuries—where young sap meets with old spine wood—and such premature budding is local, around the injury, not all over the tree. I give (and retain) this saying for future observation.'

LYNDHURST AND BROCKENHURST

Of Brook and Bramshaw we have nothing more to say than what we have already said. We think though that a word or two more about Stony Cross may well be added while dealing with this part of the Forest. They are practical words dealing with hotels and their charges.

First comes the airy ' Compton Arms,' with such luxuries as ' running water ' in nearly every bedroom, and a kindly management which packs up lunches for the walker and understands the importance such matters as early rising have in his eyes. There are hacks and hunters to be had from the hotel stables, and loose boxes for your own beasts should you bring them along too. The terms are from 5½ guineas a week *en pension*.

Just over the way is ' Dick Turpin's Cottage,' where they take visitors from 2½ to 3½ guineas a week ' according to room and season.' It is a tiny place run by cheerful people who assure us that they thoroughly understand the needs of the walker and like dealings with him.

Not the least of the blessings shared by these two houses is that the 'buses pass their doors.

For those who prefer to use Lyndhurst or Brockenhurst as their base we set down the names and charges of various hotels, culled from the *Automobile Association's Handbook 1933–4.*

Lyndhurst has ' The Crown,' from 7s. 6d. (all the figures we mention deal with the price of single rooms per night); ' The Grand,' from 8s. 6d. ; and ' The Stag,' from 4s. 6d.

Brockenhurst has the ' Balmer Lawn Hotel,' from 8s. 6d.; and the ' Forest Park,' from 6s. 6d. Personally I feel it might be nice to stay at the ' Olde Tea House Private

Hotel,' where hangs the portrait of the noble Slut. The terms for the summer are from 3 guineas a week.

Here we wish to make good a grave omission by speaking about Brockenhurst's church. In its walls are traces of Saxon as well as Norman masonry, its great square font is Norman, and its chancel is thirteenth century. The south doorway has fine Norman carving, and not far from it is a great healthy yew said to have been growing here at the time of the Conquest.

In a window of the north aisle are two squares of modern glass which seem to me so good that I cannot pass them without mention. The subject of one is a ship with a saint aboard her ; she is sailing towards a most attractive sun, her sails filled with the airs blown by an obliging cherub. The other window has heraldry, a map of the world, and a flag worked into a harmonious and charming design.

We have now told all we know about the New Forest and take our leave of our readers, hoping that if they follow any of the routes that we have set down they will enjoy them as much as we did.

Mr. Bundy can say farewell as perkily as he cried ' Hail,' but with Bill this is not so. The reason is a sad one. He was attacked some weeks ago by a plucky but ill-advised fox terrier, and instead of, as is his custom, merely rolling the offender over he dealt with it severely. Alas ! about a month later he saw the dog again, and I am ashamed to say attacked it on sight. The results were as follows—a badly mauled ear for the fox terrier, a hasty visit to the police station by its agitated mistress, and the arrival at our house that same evening of a tall policeman with a twinkle in his eye and a request for an interview with Bill. Bill greeted him with every mark of affection but was duly cautioned, and has now been made to understand that if he is not *very* careful he may find himself doing time in a suit of broad arrows ! Thus, as he bows he blushes.

INDEX

INDEX

INDEX

Pig Bush, 217, 220.
Pignal Enclosure, 135.
Pignalhill Enclosure, 135.
pigs, 217-220.
Pilley Bailey, 240.
,,   Street, 240.
pines, 73, 80, 92.
Pinnick, 8, 9, 12.
Piper's Weight, 70, 100.
Pitts Wood, 60, 63.
Plain Heath, 231.
poaching, 185-186.
pollarding, 145.
ponies, 10, 64, 79, 101-4, 110,
    111, 236-7.
,,   owners' pride in, 80.
Pontoise, John of, 138.
potteries, 28, 29, 58, 254.
Poulner, 23, 234.
Pound Heath, 179.
Pound Hill Gate, 114.
Poundhill Heath, 134.
Prophete, John, 249.
Puckpits, 113, 114.
Purkis, 92.
Puttles Bridge, 130.

Quadrille Court, 255.
Queen Beeches, 53, 109.
Queen Bower, 134.
Queen's Head Hotel, 101, 104.

Ramnor Enclosure, 142.
redshanks, 204, 208, 211.
Redshoot, 6, 8, 9, 12, 14.
Rhinefield Lodge, 128, 129.
,,   Sandys, 231.
,,   Walk, 128, 165.
Ridley Plain, 11.
,,   Wood, 145, 150, 239.
ringed plovers, 209.
Ringwood, 4, 12, 14, 22, 100, 152,
    153, 246, 248, 249.
Ripley, 238.
,,   North, 239.
roadside shag, 67.
Rockbourne, 246.

Rockford Common, 6, 7, 12, 14,
    18, 21, 23, 32, 233.
Roe Cottage, 8, 9, 18, 243.
,,   Wood, 8, 14, 18, 19, 233, 243.
roosters, quarrelsome, 177-9.
Rose, Stewart, 252.
Royal Oak, 36, 77, 86.
Roydon Farm, 169, 172.
,,   Wood, 169.
Rufus, William, 92, 93.
,,   Stone, the, 93, 94.

St. Leonards Barn, 205.
,,   Chapel, 205.
,,   Grange, 204, 216,
        241.
Salisbury Cathedral, 70.
,,   Trench Wood, 72, 89.
salmon, 20, 248.
Sandford, 239.
Sandyballs, 64.
saltmarshes, 204, 206.
Scott, Sir Walter, 153, 192, 252,
    253.
Setley Plain, 166, 240, 255.
Setthorns, 164, 165, 166.
shade, 95.
Shappen Bottom, 158, 159.
shellduck, 198-9, 211, 212, 221.
Shirley, 238.
Skers Farm, 91.
Sloden Enclosure, 29, 31, 37, 43,
        44.
,,   Old, 39, 42, 43, 44, 45,
        48, 75, 76, 78.
Slufters, 78, 112.
smooth snake, 146.
snipe, 28, 201.
Solent, the, 3, 165, 209, 210, 211,
    241.
Somerley, 6.
Sopley, 246, 250.
Southampton, 230.
,,   Docks, 201.
,,   Water, 3, 242, 256.
Southey, 167, 168, 251.
Sowley Pond, 212, 213, 240, 255.

Milton Keynes UK
Ingram Content Group UK Ltd.
UKHW030624080924
1541UKWH00033B/168